Currency Options

CURRENCY OPTIONS

Brian Coyle

Glenlake Publishing Company, Ltd
Chicago • London • New Delhi

AMACOM
American Management Association
New York • Atlanta • Boston • Chicago • Kansas City • San Francisco • Washington, D.C.
Brussels • Mexico City • Tokyo • Toronto

This book is available at a special
discount when ordered in bulk quantities.
For information contact Special Sales Department,
AMACOM, an imprint of AMA Publications, a division of
American Management Association,
1601 Broadway, New York, NY 10019

ISBN: 0-8144-0613-0

Printing number

10 9 8 7 6 5 4 3 2 1

Contents

1

Introduction

The foreign exchange markets exist for buying and selling currencies. One currency is exchanged for another at a specified rate of exchange in a spot (immediate) or a forward transaction. Spot and forward transactions are sufficient for many of the foreign exchange requirements of companies, investors and banks that have receipts or payments in foreign currencies.

However, as the foreign exchange markets have grown and developed, more sophisticated financial instruments have been devised, partly as an alternative to forward exchange transactions. These instruments are derived from an underlying FX transaction and are called derivative instruments or derivatives. They include currency options, futures and swaps.

Options are the subject of this section that aims to explain what they are, how they are bought and sold, why they are used, and who uses them.

Features of Currency Options

An option is an agreement between two counterparties, giving the option buyer or option holder, the right, but not the obligation, either to buy or to sell a quantity of an item at a fixed price, on or before a specified date in the future. If the option is exercised, the option writer is obliged to sell or to buy the item on the terms specified in the option. The purchase cost of an option is called the premium.

An option's key feature is the choice that the option holder is given

- whether to exercise the right to buy or sell the underlying item at the fixed price, or
- whether to do nothing and allow the option to lapse at expiry.

Options are written for a variety of items, including a quantity of shares, known as a stock option; a notional loan or deposit known as an interest rate option, and a quantity of currency, known as a currency option.

What is a Currency Option?

A currency option gives its holder the right, but not the obligation, either to buy from the option writer, or to sell to the option writer, a stated quantity of one currency in exchange for another,

- at a fixed rate of exchange, known variously as the strike price, exercise price or exercise rate
- on a given future date, or at any time up to and including a given future date.

The option holder pays a premium to the option writer when the option is written.

Currency Option

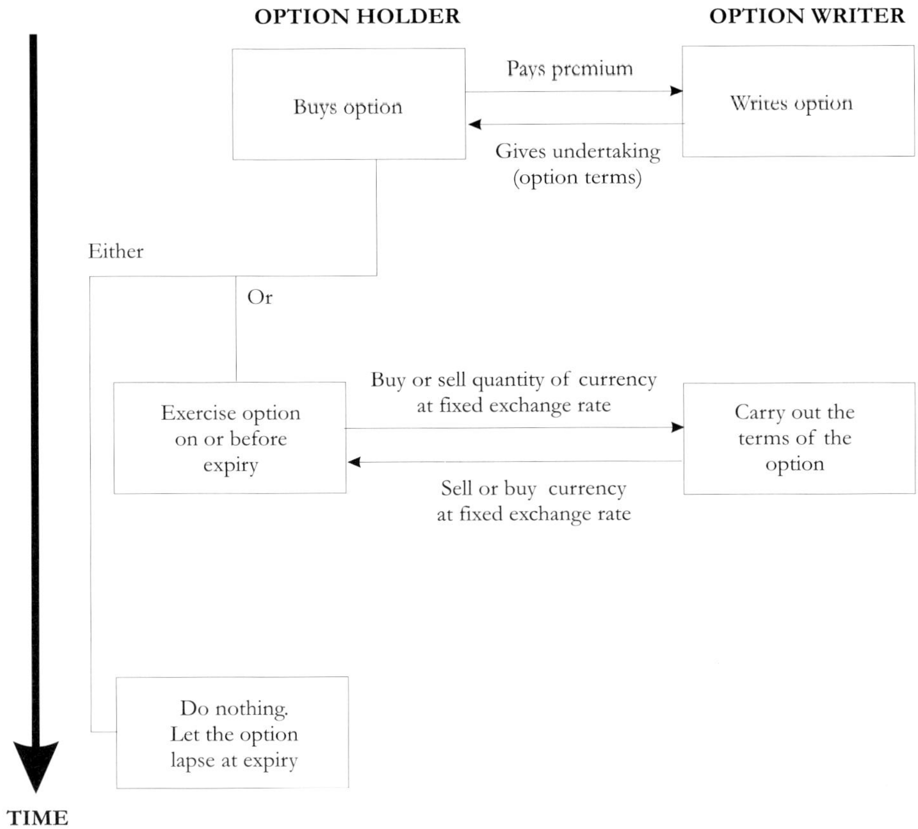

Currency Option

For example, a company could purchase an option from a bank to sell SFr200,000 in exchange for sterling at a rate of SFr2.45 on June 28.

Specifications of a Currency Option

A currency option is an agreement, confirmed in writing that must specify

- the counterparties, the option holder and the option writer
- the underlying currencies
- whether the option gives its holder the right to buy or to sell one of the underlying currencies in exchange for the other

- the amount of currency
- the exchange rate, or strike price
- the expiry date
- whether the option can be exercised on that date only, or at any time up to that date
- in the case of over-the-counter options, whether the option is on the spot or the forward currency
- the premium
- the method of settlement, if the option is exercised.

Over-the-counter Options and Traded Options

The counterparties to an option are the option holder (buyer) and the option writer (seller). Options can be purchased from two sources.

- Over-the-counter options (OTC options) are negotiated between a customer and a bank. The customer can be a non-bank organization or another bank. The bank agrees to write the option whose specifications are tailored to the customer's particular requirements. The bank also establishes the purchase price (premium) the customer must pay.
- Traded options are written and purchased on an options exchange, and subsequently can be re-sold and re-purchased secondhand up to their expiry date. Traded options are similar in most respects to OTC options, but they have standardized specifications and are available for certain currencies only.

The Underlying Currencies and Currency Amounts
An OTC currency option can be arranged for any underlying currencies, provided that the customer can find a bank that is willing to write the option. A customer could have difficulty arranging an option involving an illiquid or exotic currency; terms for a currency that is not widely traded on the FX markets.

Exchange-traded options are available only for specific pairs of currencies.

An OTC option can be written for any amount of currency, although a typical option could be to buy or sell around $20 million or its equivalent value for another currency. Exchange-traded options are for standard, specific quantities of a currency.

An option specifies the amount of one currency and the fixed exchange rate (strike price). The amount of the second currency then can be calculated. For example, if an option is exercised to sell €100,000 in exchange for dollars at a strike price of €1 = $1.06, the writer of the option will have to buy the euros for $106,000.

Call Options and Put Options

Options are either calls or puts.

A call option gives its holder the right to *purchase* a specified quantity of one currency in exchange for another currency. For example, an option to buy $500,000 in exchange for sterling is a call on dollars against sterling. Similarly, an option to buy Swiss francs in exchange for dollars is a call on Swiss francs against dollars.

A put option gives the holder the right to *sell* a specified quantity of one currency in exchange for another. For example, an option to sell $200,000 in exchange for euros is a put on dollars against euros or a dollar put against euros.

The writer of a call option must sell the currency to the option holder if the option is exercised, and the writer of a put option must buy the currency from the option holder if the option is exercised, at the exchange rate (strike price) in the option agreement.

Strike Price

The exchange rate specified in the option agreement is known variously as the strike price, strike rate or exercise price. This rate might be above, below or the same as the current spot exchange rate when the option is purchased.

When an option is arranged between a bank and its customer, the strike price is negotiable. The customer will specify the required strike price, and the bank will quote a premium that takes into account, among other things, the difference between the strike price and current market exchange rates.

For exchange-traded options there are several available strike prices, some above and some below the current spot rate. These available prices are specified by the options exchange authorities. The amount of premium will vary according to the difference between the strike price and the current spot rate of exchange.

Expiry Date

An option expires after a specified time on a specified date. If it is not exercised by this time, it lapses.

OTC options can be written for any expiry date, provided the date is a bank working day.

Exchange traded options are written for specific expiry dates. For example, all options written on an exchange for expiry in September will expire on the same day in September.

American and European Options

An option must specify an expiration date.

- An American option allows the holder to exercise the option at any time up to and including its expiry date.

- A European option allows the holder to exercise the option on its expiry date only.

The terms American and European are misleading because both styles of option are used in all countries where options are traded, and for practical purposes there is no difference between the US and Europe. However, because American options give greater flexibility to the option holder, they are more expensive to buy.

Options on the Spot and the Forward

An option can be

- on the spot currency, or
- on the forward currency (OTC options only).

An option on the spot currency is an option on a spot currency transaction. An option on the forward currency is an option on a forward contract.

Example
A company purchases two call options on dollars against sterling, each with a three-month maturity.

- One is a European dollar call on a spot strike price of £1 = $1.5930.
- The other is a European dollar call on a three-month forward strike price of £1 = $1.5930.

When the options were purchased, the spot rate was $1.6000 and the three-month forward rate was $1.5930.

Analysis
The call option on the spot currency gives the holder the right to buy dollars at $1.5930 at maturity. This option was out-of-the-money by $0.0070 when written.

The call option on the forward currency gives the company the right to enter a three-month forward contract, at the option's maturity, to buy dollars at a rate of 1.5930. This option was at-the-money-forward (ATMF) when written.

Option Premium

An option is purchased from an option writer at a price that is called a premium. This will be paid at the time of purchase, or very soon after, in the currency specified in the option agreement. The premium is expressed

- as a monetary fraction of each unit of the option's underlying currency amount such as x cents per euro, or
- as a percentage of the underlying amount.

Examples
If a company buys a call option on $250,000 against euros, and the premium is 0.8 euros per dollar, the premium payment will be €2,000 (0.0080 x 250,000).

Similarly, if a company buys a put option on SFr250,000 against sterling at a strike price of £1 = SFr2.50 and the premium is payable in Swiss francs at 1.5% of the underlying amount, the premium payment will be SFr13,750 (1.5% of 250,000).

Exercise and Settlement

If an option is exercised there must be a settlement of amounts due between the option holder and the option writer. Arrangements for settlement are specified in the option agreement.

Exercising an Option
An option will be exercised only if it benefits the option holder to do so rather than to let the option lapse.

An option on the spot currency will be exercised only if the strike price is more favorable than the spot rate in the FX market on the exercise date.

A put option will be exercised only if it enables the option holder to buy the currency at the option strike price for less than it would cost to buy at the spot rate in the FX market, i.e. the option holder can sell the currency the put refers to at a higher price than current spot rate.

Example 1
On June 7 a company buys a call option from its bank for the purchase of $60,000 in exchange for sterling at a strike price of £1 = $1.55, for exercise on September 25.

Analysis
If the option is exercised, it will cost the option holder £38,709.68 ($60,000 ÷ 1.55) to buy the $60,000.

- If the spot exchange rate on September 25 is above 1.55, at 1.60 for example, the option holder will not exercise the option because it would be £1,209.68 cheaper to purchase the required $60,000 from the bank for £37,500 at the spot rate ($60,000 ÷ 1.60). The option holder is not obliged to exercise the option, and in this situation would let it lapse.
- If the spot exchange rate on September 25 is below $1.55, at $1.50 for example, the option holder will exercise the option and buy the $60,000 for £38,709.68 from the bank. Purchasing the dollars in the spot market would cost £40,000 ($60,000 ÷ 1.50) that is £1,290.32 more. The option holder could exercise the option to buy the dollars, then resell them immediately at a profit.

Example 2
On March 16, a company buys a European put option from its bank for the sale of €600,000 against dollars at an exercise rate of €1 = $1.0800, for expiry on June 10.

Analysis
If the option is exercised, the company will sell the euros to the bank for $648,000 (600,000 x 1.08).

- If the spot exchange rate on June 10 is below 1.08, at €1 = $1.05, the option holder will exercise the option. Selling €600,000 at the spot rate would earn just $630,000 (600,000 ÷ 1.05) that is $18,000 less than the company could earn by exercising the option. The option holder could buy euros in the spot market and resell them at a profit by exercising the option.
- If the spot exchange rate on June 10 is above 1.08, €1 = $1.10, the option will not be exercised. The company could earn more by selling the €600,000 at the spot rate, for $660,000.

Settlement
OTC options normally are settled two business days after the option has been exercised. The arrangements for settlement vary according to whether the option holder is a bank or a non-bank organization.

- If the option holder is a bank, the option usually will be settled by an exchange of currencies between nominated bank accounts, i.e. the option is exercised into an underlying spot FX transaction.
- If the option holder is not a bank, the option writer usually will prefer to make a cash payment in settlement of the difference between the option strike price and the spot rate of exchange at the exercise date. The option holder and the option writer agree the spot rate and a cash payment is made, usually two business days later, to the option holder's nominated account.

Example
A call option on C$1 million against sterling has a strike price of £1 = C$2. The option is exercised on Friday October 21.

Analysis
If the option holder were a bank, it would be normal for settlement to be arranged by

- the option holder paying £500,000 (C$1 million ÷ 2) into an account nominated by the option writer, possibly in London
- the option writer paying C$1 million into an account nominated by the option holder, possibly in Toronto.

Delivery would take place two business days after exercise, on Tuesday October 25.

If the option holder were a non-bank corporate, the option could provide for cash settlement if the option were exercised. Suppose, for example, that when the option is exercised, the holder and the writer agree that the spot rate is £1= C$1.90. The option writer would pay the difference between the cost of the C$1 million at the strike price of 2.00 and the cost at the spot rate of 1.90.

	£
Cost of C$1 million at £1 = C$2.00	500,000.00
Cost of C$1 million at £1 = C$1.90	526,315.79
Difference	26,315.79

The option normally would be settled by the delivery of £26,315.79 by the option writer into a nominated account of the option holder, on Tuesday October 25.

When a currency option is settled by exchanging the full amounts in each currency, the option writer is exposed to *delivery risk*, i.e. there is a risk that the option holder could fail to make his currency payment two days after exercising the option. By arranging cash settlement of an option, delivery risk is avoided because the option writer makes a payment to the option holder only for the net amount owed.

Currency Options and Forward Contracts

A currency option is an instrument that allows the option holder to fix a worst possible rate of exchange for a specified amount of currency at some time in the future. A forward exchange contract is an alternative instrument that can be used to buy or sell a specified amount of currency at a fixed rate of exchange, at some time in the future.

Because both instruments can be used to secure a forward rate of exchange, it is useful to compare them and to highlight key differences.

Features of Options and Forward Contracts

Currency option	*Forward contract*
A currency option does not bind the option holder to buy or sell the currency.	A foreign exchange contract is a binding agreement to buy or sell the currency.
An option is therefore for the *conditional* future sale or purchase of a specified quantity of one currency in exchange for another.	A forward contract is therefore for the *unconditional* future sale or purchase of a specified quantity of one currency in exchange for another.
An option is arranged between an option writer and the option buyer (option holder). The option writer could be a bank.	A forward contract is between a bank and a customer.
An option is agreed individually between a bank and a customer. Alternatively, it is purchased and sold on a traded options exchange.	A forward contract is agreed individually between a bank and a customer.
The exchange rate, or strike price, is specified or fixed in the option agreement.	The exchange rate is specified or fixed in the contract. It is based on the spot rate, plus or minus a forward adjustment to allow for interest rate differentials between the two currencies.

An option must be purchased from the option writer at a price, known as a premium.	A forward contract is not purchased. The bank's profit comes from the spread between its buying and selling prices for trading in the currency.
An option is exercised by the option holder giving notice to the option writer.	A forward contract must be settled by both parties.

Exercises

To check your understanding of the basic features of currency options, attempt the following exercises. Assume in every case that the company purchasing the option is large enough to be able to sell or buy foreign currency in the FX markets at the spot rate of exchange. The solutions follow.

Exercise 1

A US company has to make a payment in Swiss francs of SFr200,000 to a supplier in six months' time. To cover this transaction it wishes to purchase an option from its bank at a strike price of $1 = SFr1.60.

- Would it purchase a Swiss franc put or a Swiss franc call option?
- If the spot rate on expiry of the option is SFr1.65, would the company choose to exercise the option?

Solution

The company wishes to buy Swiss francs in exchange for dollars in order to make the payment. Therefore it will purchase a call option on SFr200,000.

At the strike price of 1.60, the purchase of SFr200,000 would cost $125,000. At the spot rate of 1.65 the cost would be less ($121,212.12). The company will let the option lapse and purchase the Swiss francs from its bank at the spot rate.

Exercise 2

A UK company expects to receive $400,000 in three months' time from a customer in the middle east, and wishes to cover this transaction by purchasing an option from its bank at a strike price of £1 = $1.6100.

- Would it purchase a dollar put or a call option?
- What would it cost if the premium were $0.0025 per $1?
- If, on the expiry date of the option, the exchange rate is £1 = $1.6400 and the company receives $600,000, rather than the expected $400,000, would it choose to exercise to the option? What other action would it take to convert the dollars into sterling?

Solution

The company will be selling its dollar receipts to obtain sterling, and so will buy a put option on $400,000.

At a premium of £0.0025 per dollar, the full purchase price of the option is £1,000 (£0.0025 x 400,000).

At a strike price of 1.61, the company would exercise its option because this is a more favorable rate for selling than the spot rate of 1.64, i.e. it will earn more in sterling by selling $400,000 at 1.61 than at the 1.64 spot rate. The option is for just $400,000, however, and the extra income of $200,000 will be sold at the spot rate.

	£
Proceeds from exercising the option ($400,000 ÷ 1.61)	248,447.20
Proceeds from spot sale of additional income ($200,000 ÷ 1.64)	121,951.21
Total sterling proceeds from $600,000	370,398.41

Exercise 3

A company expects to make a payment of €500,000 in seven months' time, and wishes to cover this transaction by purchasing a European-style euro option against dollars from its bank at a strike price of £1 = $1.04. On the expiry date, the spot rate is €1 = $1.0725 – 1.0735, but the company now finds that the payment in euros is no longer required. What should the company do with the option?

Solution

The company expected to purchase €500,000 and would have arranged a euro call option on this amount at the strike price of 1.04. On expiry date, the strike price is more favorable than the spot price, and although the company does not require the €500,000, it can make a profit by exercising the option.

Suppose the option writer (bank) and the company agree that the spot price at the time of exercising the option is 1.0725.

	$
Exercise option: buy €500,000 at €1 = $1.04	-520,000
Sell €500,000 at spot rate of $1.0725	+ 536,250
Profit	16,250

In practise, the option would probably be settled for cash, with a payment of $16,250 from the option writer to the company.

Summary

The main features of currency options are

- a currency option confers a right on its buyer, rather than an obligation
- a call option gives its buyer the right to buy a specified quantity of one currency in exchange for another at a pre-determined rate of exchange, the strike price or exercise price.
- a put option gives its buyer the right to sell a specified quantity of one currency in exchange for another, at a specified rate of exchange
- over-the-counter (OTC) options are negotiated between the option buyer and a bank that agrees to write the option in return for a premium. Options also can be purchased and sold on an options exchange
- the process of an option holder activating the right is called exercising the option.

- European options can be exercised on a specific date. US options, that are more expensive to buy, can be exercised at any time up to and including a specific date. An option lapses if it is not exercised by its expiry date.
- when an option is exercised, settlement takes place typically two business days later, either by means of an exchange of currencies between the option writer and the option holder, or by means of a payment (cash settlement) by the option writer to the option holder for the net amount owed.

The OTC market in currency options is large. Option writers, mostly banks, will write options with amounts, maturities and other features tailored to the requirements of their customers. On the other hand, traded options are less flexible and less commonly used because they are standardized contracts.

The Risks and Potential Gains

Currency options must be attractive to both their purchasers and writers; they wouldn't be bought and sold otherwise.

The Option Holder

Purchasers of options are banks and non-bank organizations. The principal attractions of an option to its holder are that

- the option secures a worst-case exchange rate for buying or selling currency that can be used if a better rate cannot be obtained at the appropriate time in the foreign exchange spot market
- the holder is not obliged to exercise the option.

It is important to recognize that in many cases an option will not be exercised because the strike price of the option is less favorable than the rate obtainable for a spot transaction in the foreign exchange market.

Compared with the alternative of not buying an option, the maximum extra cost, or loss, for the option holder is the premium paid to the option writer. This maximum loss occurs if the option is not exercised and it is a cost that the option holder is willing to risk.

A significant benefit to the option holder is the protection or insurance that an option provides by securing a worst-case rate of exchange. It can be helpful to compare a currency option with an insurance policy. The buyer of travel accident insurance, for example, pays a premium to obtain the insurance cover, but will make a claim against the insurance company only if a travel accident occurs. The policyholder will prefer not to have to make a claim rather than to have an accident. In the same way, an option holder will prefer the spot rate of exchange at expiry to be more favorable than the option's strike price, i.e. to be better than the worst-case rate of exchange that the option guarantees.

In measuring the gain or loss to an option holder from buying an option, it is usual to compare what the income or cost to the option holder would be of

- buying an option and paying a premium, and
- not buying an option, and buying or selling the required amount of currency at the available spot rate of exchange at the appropriate time.

It is also possible to compare the cost of buying an option with the cost of arranging a forward exchange contract, but this method of measuring the gain or loss from an option is less common.

Example 1

A US company arranges a European call option on €200,000 against dollars at a strike price of €1 = $1.05, with an expiry date of June 15. The premium for the option is $2,200, payable in dollars.

Option Holder's Gain or Loss
(Option vs. Spot Transaction)

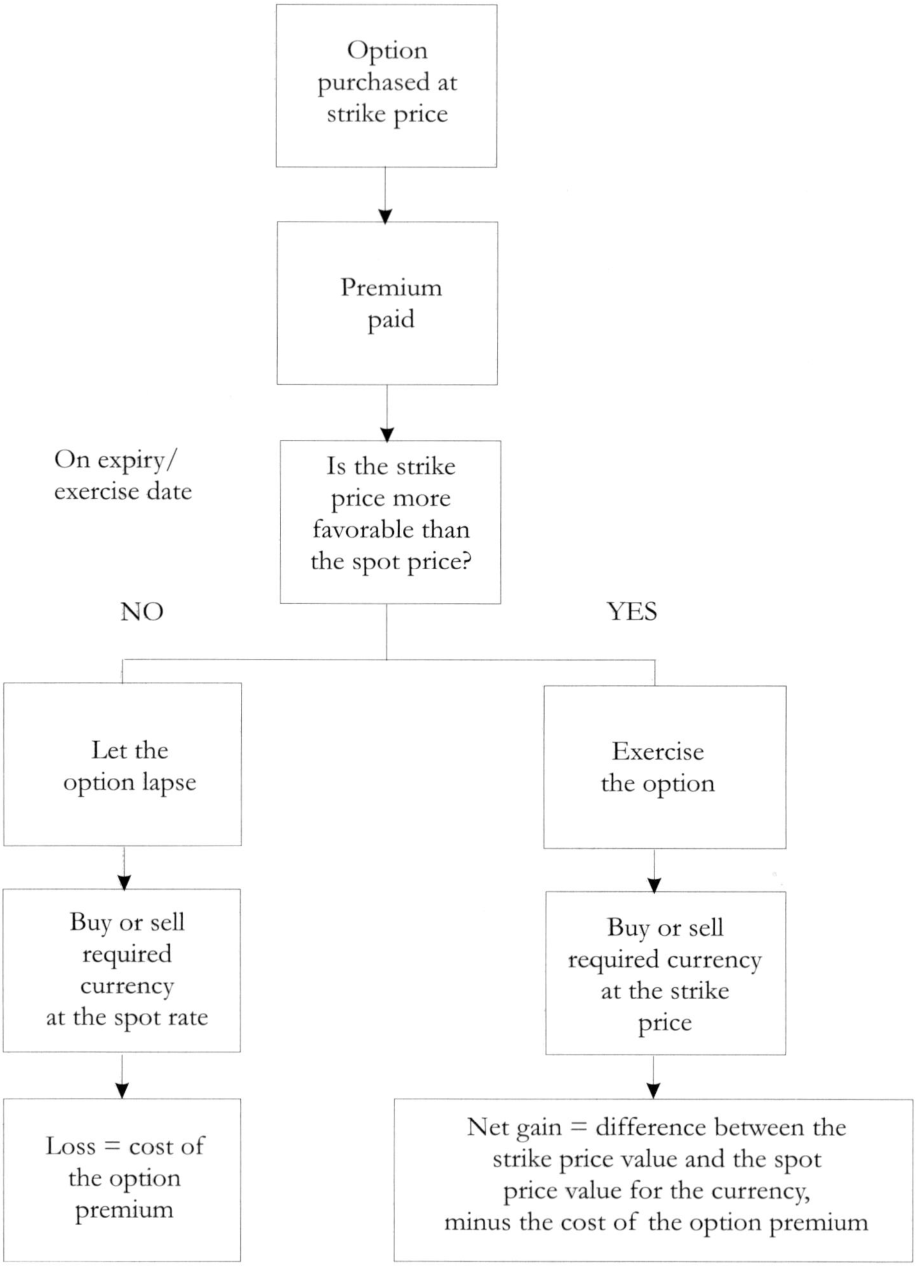

On June 15, the available spot rate for buying euros is €1 = $1.07. The company requires the €200,000 to pay a supplier for goods purchased.

Analysis

The strike price is more favorable than the spot rate, and the company will exercise the option to buy euros at $1.05. The lower cost (net gain) from using the more advantageous strike price is the difference in total cost between the two rates, minus the premium paid for the option.

	$
Cost of €200,000 at 1.05	-210,000
Cost of €200,000 at 1.07	214,000
Gain from exercise of option	4,000
Premium cost	-2,200
Net gain	1,800

Example 2

Taking the same situation as in Example 1, suppose that the spot rate on June 15 was

€1 = $1.0600
€1 = $1.0450

Analysis

Spot rate $1.06. The strike price is more favorable than the spot rate and the option will be exercised. The gain on the difference between the two exchange rates is less than the cost of the option premium, and the option holder makes a net loss, or incurs higher costs, as follows.

	$
Cost of €200,000 at 1.06	-212,000
Cost of €200,000 at 1.07	214,000
Gain from exercise of option	2,000
Premium cost	-2,200
Net loss	-200

Spot rate $1.045. The strike price for buying euros is less favorable than the spot rate, and the company would let the option lapse, buying the €200,000 at 1.045, at a cost of $209,000. The loss, or extra cost to the option holder, is $2,200. This is the amount of premium paid for the option that has not been used.

Maximum Loss and Potential Gain to the Option Holder

The cost of the premium is the maximum loss that an option holder can suffer, compared with not buying the option and waiting to buy or sell currency at the prevailing spot rate.

In contrast, the potential net gains to the option holder are limited only by the amount that spot rates fluctuate. Returning to Example 1, if the spot rate had been €1 = $1.20 on expiry date, the net gain to the option holder, when compared with buying the euros spot, would have been $27,800 ($30,000 minus premium of $2,200).

If the spot rate were €1 = $1.20

	$
Cost of buying €200,000 at $1.05 (option strike price)	-210,000
Cost of buying €200,000 at $1.20 (spot price)	240,000
Gain from exercising the option	30,000
Cost of premium	- 2,200
Net gain	27,800

If the spot rate had been higher still, the call option holder's profit would have been even higher.

Example 3

The same analysis applies to put options.

A UK company expects to receive $3,000,000 in six months and arranges a dollar put option at a strike price of £1 = $1.50. The premium is £14,000, payable in sterling.

Analysis

If the sterling/dollar spot rate on the expiry date is below 1.50, the company will let the put option lapse and prefer to sell the dollars at the more favorable spot rate. For example, if the spot rate were £1 = $1.40, the dollars could be sold spot to earn £2,142,857.10. The option holder's loss from buying the option would be £14,000, the cost of the premium.

On the other hand, if the sterling/dollar spot rate on the expiry date were above 1.50, the company would exercise its put option. For example, if the spot rate were 1.60, it would be more profitable to sell the dollars at 1.50 under the option entitlement.

	£
Revenue from $3,000,000 at 1.50 (strike price)	2,000,000
Revenue from $3,000,000 at 1.60 (spot rate)	-1,875,000
Gain from exercising the option	125,000
Premium cost	-14,000
Net gain	111,000

The Effective Exchange Rate

The effective exchange rate that an option holder obtains for buying or selling currency incorporates the cost of the premium.

Example

A company buys a European call option on SFr2 million against sterling at a strike price of £1 = SFr2.20. The premium costs £6,000. If the spot rate on expiry date is £1 = SFr2.23, the company would let the option lapse and buy SFr2 million at the spot rate. The full cost of these transactions to the company will be

	£
Purchase of SFr2 million at £1 = SFr2.23	896,860.98
Premium	6,000.00
Total cost	902,860.98

Taking into account the cost of the premium, the effective exchange rate for the Swiss francs is £1 = SFr2.2152 (SFr2 million ÷ £902,860.98).

If the spot rate on expiry date were £1 = SFr2.18, the company would exercise the option and buy Swiss francs at the strike price of SFr2.20. The full cost of these transactions to the company is

	£
Exercise option: buy SFr2 million at 2.20	909,090.91
Premium	6,000.00
Total cost	915,090.91

The effective exchange rate is £1 = SFr2.1856 (SFr2 million ÷ £915,090.91). This is the worst-case exchange rate that the option holder has secured by purchasing the option.

The Option Writer

The seller or writer of a currency option can be either a bank or, if the option is exchange-traded, a dealer in one of the traded options markets around the world. The benefit for an option writer is the premium earned from the sale of the option. The risk is that if the option is exercised, the strike price, being more favorable to the option holder than current market exchange rates, will be less favorable to the option writer who therefore will make a loss. The option writer will be obliged to buy or sell currency at a rate that is less favorable than current rates.

The option writer's potential gains and risks are exactly the opposite of the option holder's.

- The maximum profit the option writer can earn is the premium received. This will occur whenever the option is allowed to lapse.
- When the holder exercises the option, the option writer will make a loss to set off against the premium. The loss occurs because the option writer must buy or sell currency at the strike price when spot market prices would be preferable.

Thus the option writer has an upside scope for gain that is limited to the amount of the premium income received, but an unlimited downside risk of loss that is the difference between the strike price and the exchange rate at expiry.

Option Writer's Gain or Loss

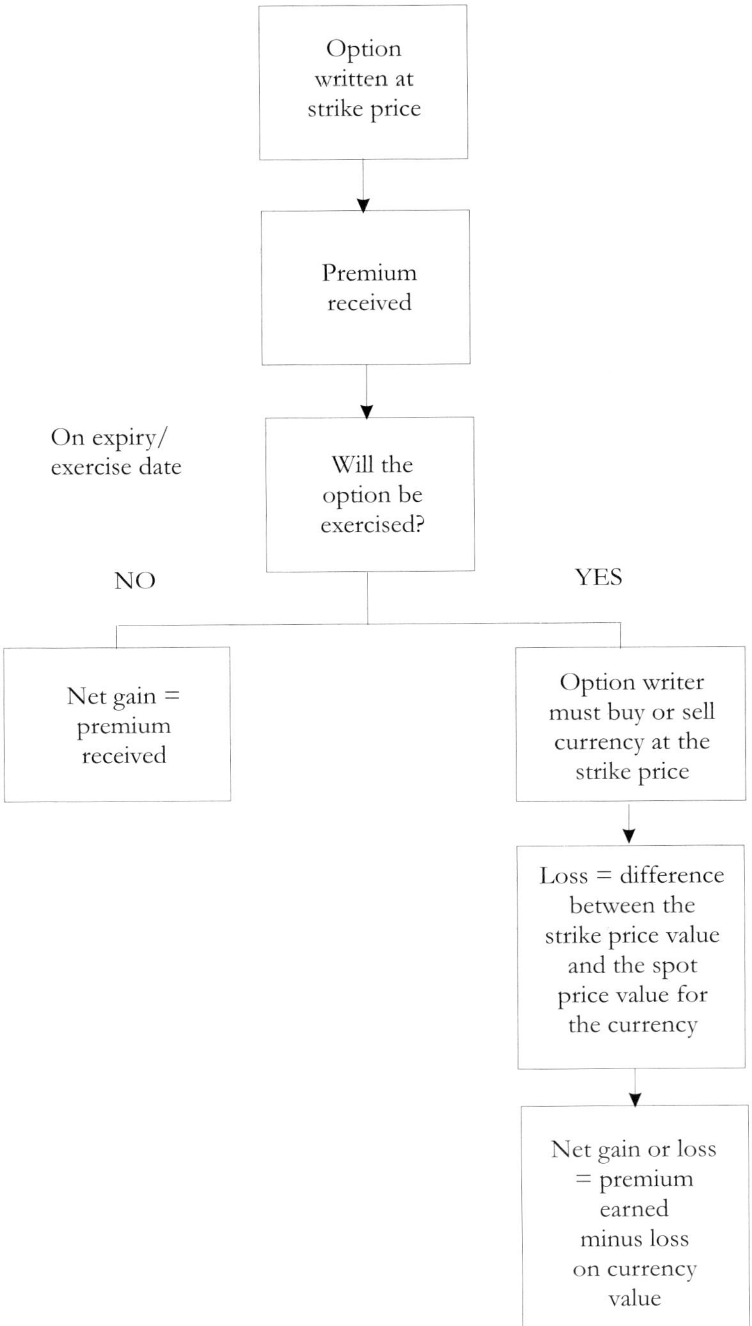

Option Writer's Loss when Option Exercised

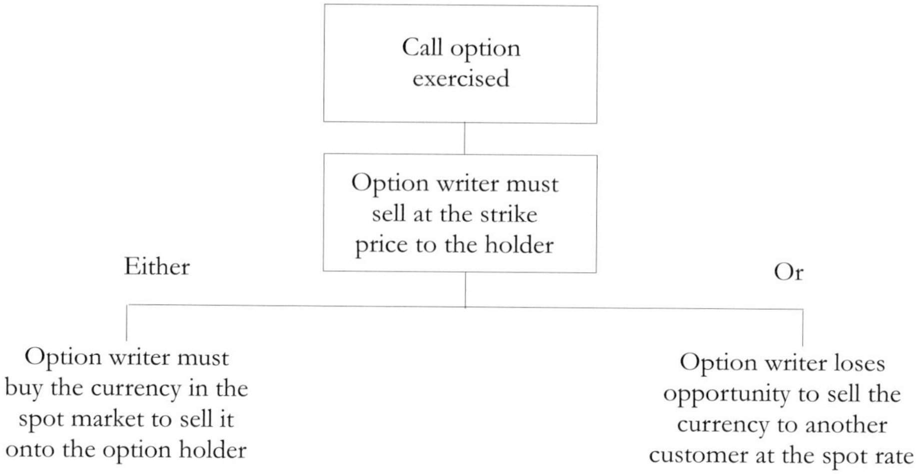

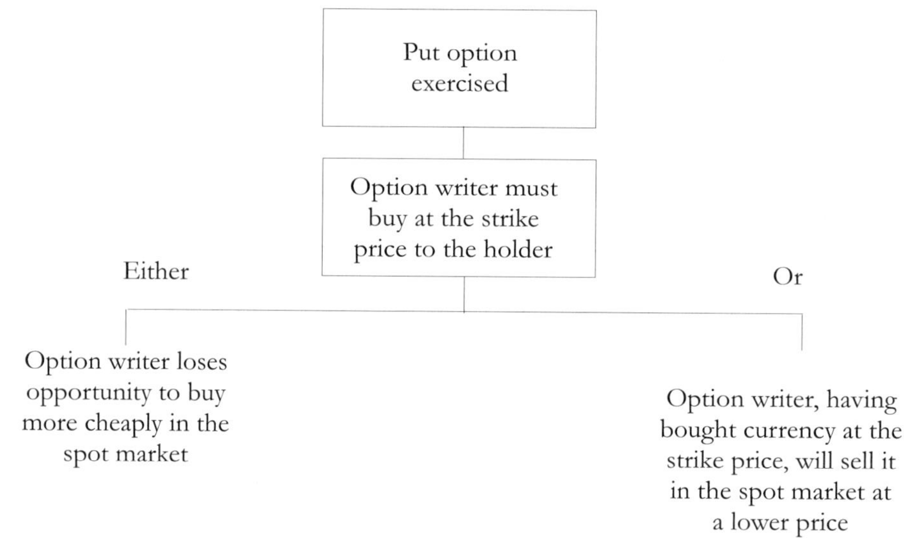

Example
A non-bank customer buys a put option on $200,000 against Swiss francs at a strike price of $1 = SFr1.70. The premium, payable in Swiss francs, is SFr1,900.

The option is exercised before expiry, and a cash settlement is paid by the option writer (bank). The spot rate of exchange for the cash settlement is SFr1.6950.

Analysis
When the option is exercised, the agreed cash settlement is

	SFr
Sale value of $200,000 at option strike price (x 1.70)	340,000
Sale value of $200,000 at spot price (x 1.695)	339,000
Cash settlement	1,000

	Option holder SFr	Option writer SFr
Cash settlement	+1,000	-1,000
Premium	-1,900	+1,900
Net gain/loss	-900	+900

Comparing the Risks and Gains of Option Holder and Option Writer
Options are an example of a zero sum game because

- if the option holder makes a gain out of exercising an option, the option writer makes an equal and matching loss, and
- if the option is allowed to lapse, the option holder's loss and the option writer's profit also are equal, being the amount of the premium paid.

This situation is shown in the diagrams.

- When the option writer makes a loss, the option holder makes an equal and matching gain. In theory, there is no limit to the size of an option holder's gain.
- The breakeven spot rate is the rate at the expiry date that would give both the option holder and the option writer neither a gain nor a loss. This is the strike price, plus in the case of call options and minus in the case of put options, an amount to allow for the premium paid to the option writer.

Example
A UK company buys a European put option on $825,000 against sterling from its bank at a strike price of £1 = $1.50. The option premium, payable in sterling, is £6,000.

If the put option is exercised, the company will sell the $825,000 to the bank at $1.50, to receive £550,000 in exchange.

	£
Put option exercised. Company receives	550,000
Deduct premium	-6,000
Net receipts	544,000

Similarly, the bank will pay £550,000, but after deducting its premium income of £6,000, its net payment will be £544,000.

The breakeven point is a spot rate at which the company could sell the $825,000 to the bank for £544,000. This is £1 = $1.5165 ($825,000 ÷ £544,000).

Call Options: Gains or Losses

Illustrative figures
Call on dollars against Swiss Francs
Amount $300,000
Strike Price $1 = SFr1.75
Premium SFr4,500

OPTION WRITER
CALL OPTION
(DOLLAR CALL)

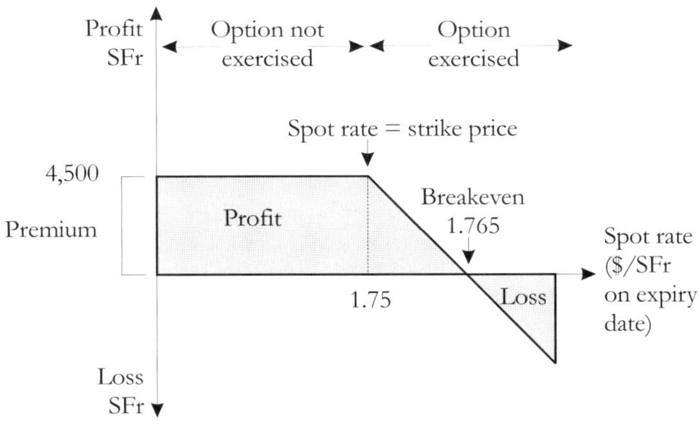

OPTION BUYER
CALL OPTION
(DOLLAR CALL)

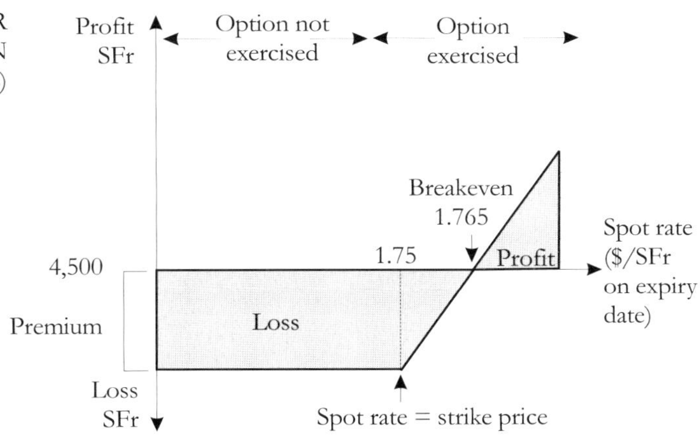

Put Options: Gains or Losses

Illustrative figures
Put on dollars against Swiss Francs
Amount $300,000
Strike Price $1 = SFr1.75
Premium SFr4,500

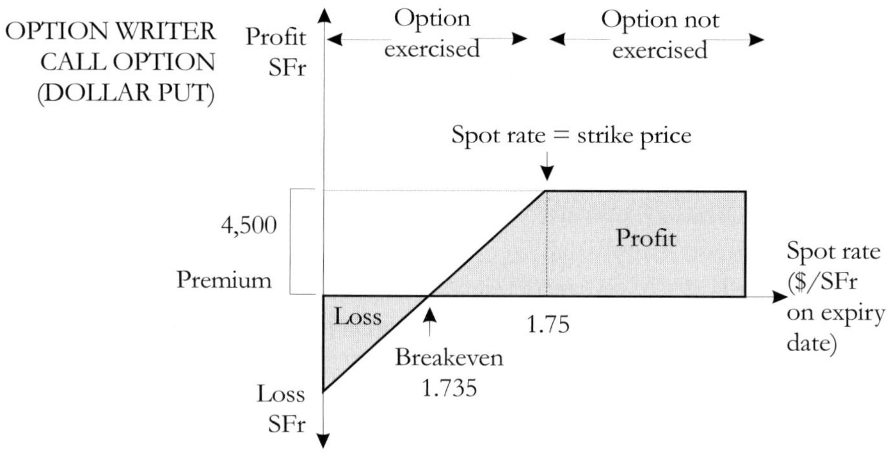

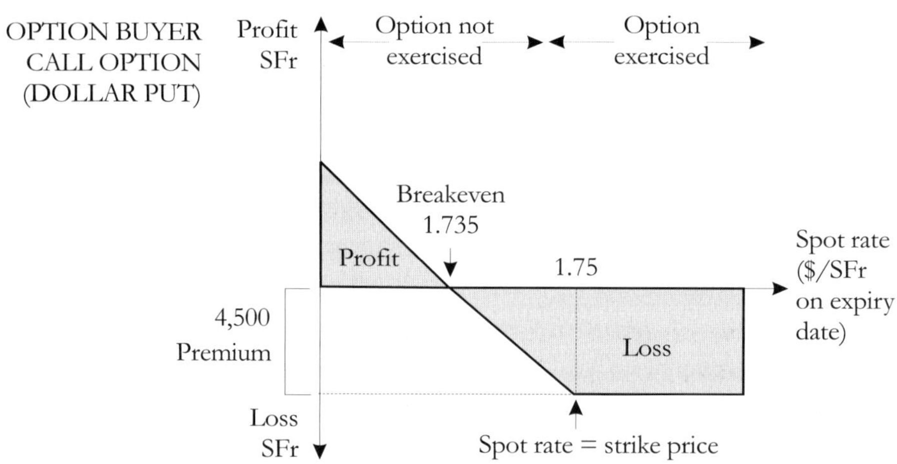

If the spot rate on expiry is $1.5165, the company will exercise its option and sell the dollars for £550,000. Its net receipts, however, would be the same as if it had not purchased an option, but waited to sell the dollars at the spot rate at the appropriate date.

The option writer (the bank) also would be at breakeven point, because it would have to buy the dollars for £550,000 when it could buy them in the spot market for £544,000; however, this loss is offset by the premium of £6,000 that it earns writing the option.

Summary

The maximum loss an option holder can incur from buying an option, and the maximum profit that an option writer can make, is the amount of the option premium. This maximum loss/gain occurs when the option is not exercised. In theory, there is no limit to the potential gain for the option holder and no limit to the potential loss for the option writer. The size of the gain or loss when an option is exercised depends on the spot exchange rate at the exercise date.

Option writers are dealers in risk who judge that their overall income from premiums will exceed their losses on the exchange rate when options are exercised. Like any business trader, a dealer in risk expects to end up in profit. This suggests that on the whole, option buyers will not make a profit from their options.

A bank or traded options market maker can try to ensure making a profit from writing options in two ways

- by charging premiums that are high enough, so that on balance gains exceed losses
- by taking measures to hedge its exposure to losses.

However, it is worth remembering that the reason for buying an option is not necessarily to make a profit. Companies might buy options to set a maximum limit to their downside risk by fixing a maximum effective purchase price or minimum effective sale price for currency. The extra cost, or loss, is considered worth paying in order to limit this risk.

Why Use Currency Options?

Primarily currency options are used in five ways

- as an alternative to forward exchange contracts for hedging currency exposure, where there is an underlying transaction creating the exposure
- for potential currency exposures
- for uncertain amounts of currency
- as a means of speculation
- to avoid utilizing a company's finite credit lines with its banks.

Hedging Currency Exposures

Currency exposures arise when a business expects to make payments or earn receipts in a foreign currency. Payments in foreign currency usually are made by purchasing the required currency in exchange for domestic currency. Similarly, foreign currency income is converted into domestic currency by selling it. The purchase or sale price for foreign currency is the rate of exchange.

Exchange rates are volatile and their movements up or down are largely unpredictable. Therefore a company that expects to pay or receive a quantity of foreign currency at some time in the future is exposed to the risk that the purchase cost will be higher or the revenue income will be lower, in domestic currency, than originally expected because of an adverse movement in the exchange rate between now and then.

Example
A UK company expects to receive $420,000 in three months that it will

convert on receipt into sterling. Currently the exchange rate is £1 = $1.50 .

Analysis

The company expects to earn £280,000 (420,000 ÷ 1.50), but the sterling/dollar rate might have moved up or down before the money is received in three months' time.

It is exposed to the risk of an adverse movement in the exchange rate during this three-month period unless it has taken measures to hedge the exposure.

- If the exchange rate in three months' time were £1 = $1.60, the company's sterling income will be only £262,500, £17,500 less than originally expected. This can be called a loss on currency movements.
- If the exchange rate in three months' time were £1 = $1.40, the company's sterling income will be £300,000 (420,000 ÷ 1.40), £20,000 more than expected. This would be regarded as a profit on currency movements.

Companies might be fully prepared to accept the risk of losses on currency movements in the belief that they will be insignificant, or that they are less likely to occur than profits. However, many companies take the view that significant exposures to currency risk ought to be minimized or avoided. Taking measures to avoid or reduce currency exposures is referred to as *hedging* the exposures.

Options vs. Forward Contracts

Forward exchange contracts are a widely used method of hedging a currency exposure because they lock in a fixed exchange rate for a future foreign currency transaction. Currency options are an alternative method of hedging currency exposure.

A currency option enables the option holder to

- lock in a worst-case exchange rate to avoid the risk of an adverse movement in the rate, and at the same time

- benefit from any favorable movement in the exchange rate by choosing not to exercise the option, and instead buying or selling the currency at the available spot rate on expiry.

Options might be preferred when there is an expectation that the exchange rate is more likely to move one way, up or down, rather than the other way. If the spot rate moves favorably, it will be cheaper to buy or more profitable to sell currency at the spot rate rather than at a pre-determined fixed forward rate. However, as a hedge against the risk that expectations could prove to be wrong, and that the spot rate will move adversely, a currency option can be purchased to secure a worst-case exchange rate. The cost of this risk protection is the option premium.

It is interesting to compare the costs of a currency option and a forward contract as alternative methods of hedging a currency exposure for a specific underlying transaction. If the strike price for a currency option is the same as the forward exchange rate for the tenor of the option, i.e. with the same maturity date as the option's expiry, comparisons about cost can be made.

Example
A UK company will receive €400,000 from a customer in three months' time. It expects the euro to strengthen against sterling over this period, but would like to construct a hedge against the risk of a weaker euro. A three-month forward contract would be obtainable at €1 = £0.6500. A euro put option on €400,000 with an expiry date in three months would have a premium cost of $5,000.

Would it be more beneficial to hedge with an option or with a forward contract?

Analysis
The hedging method that is more profitable can be determined only with hindsight.

A forward contract to sell €400,000 at £0.65 would guarantee an income of £260,000. A euro put option with an at-the-money-forward strike price of £0.65 would guarantee a worst-case income of £260,000 less the premium of £5,000 that is £255,000 net. A forward contract would be more profitable unless the net income from hedging with an option is £260,000 or more. This means that the €400,000 must have a sale value of at least £265,000 at the spot rate on expiry of the option to cover the premium cost of £5,000 and leave income of at least £260,000 for it to be more profitable than a forward contract. The breakeven spot rate on expiry is therefore €1 = £0.6625 (£265,000 ÷ €400,000).

- If the spot rate on expiry were higher than £0.6625, the option holder would let the put option lapse and sell the €400,000 spot, to earn in excess of £265,000.
- If the spot rate on expiry were below 0.6625, but above £0.65, the strike price, the option holder would let the put option lapse and sell the euros at the spot rate to earn somewhere between £260,000 and £265,000. After deducting the premium cost of £5,000, net income will be less than £260,000, and in retrospect a forward contract would have been a better hedging method.
- If the spot rate on expiry were below £0.65, the strike price, the option holder would exercise the put option and sell the euros for £260,000 to earn just £255,000, the worst-case outcome, after deducting the premium cost.

A company that chooses to purchase an option instead of arranging a forward contract normally will expect movements in the spot rate up to expiry date to be large, and that the eventual spot rate is likely to be more favorable than the rate currently obtainable for a forward exchange contract. Unless there is an assumption of a volatile exchange rate, the cost of an option premium would make options more expensive than forward contracts. *Volatility* in exchange rate movements can add to the appeal of currency options as a hedging instrument, although greater volatility is likely to mean higher premiums for the purchase of options.

Potential Currency Exposures

Currency options can be a much more attractive instrument than forward contracts when there is uncertainty about whether a future receipt or payment of currency will occur.

If a German company thinks that it will have to pay $800,000 in three months' time, it can arrange a forward contract to buy $800,000. But even if the payment isn't needed, the company is still obliged to buy the $800,000. Instead of hedging a currency exposure for a dollar payment, it has taken on an exposure for an $800,000 purchase, and will make a gain or loss accordingly when the bank closes out the forward contract.

Forward contracts can create exposures, instead of hedging them, in situations where future currency receipts or payments might not occur. Currency options get round this problem. For the cost of the premium, a company can

- let the option lapse if the receipt or payment of currency doesn't occur, or sell the option back to the bank, or in the case of exchange-traded options it may sell the option back to the market
- let the option lapse if the receipt or payment does occur, but the strike price is less favorable than the spot rate
- exercise the option if the receipt or payment does occur, and the strike price is more favorable than the spot rate.

In addition, even if the receipt or payment does not occur, but the strike price is more favorable than the spot rate, the opportunity will arise to make an immediate profit by exercising the option and arranging a reverse transaction at the spot FX market rate.

- For a call option, the option holder could exercise the right to purchase the currency at the strike price and sell it immediately at the higher spot rate.
- For a put option, the option holder could buy currency at the spot rate to coincide with exercising the right to sell it at a higher strike price.

Alternatively, the option holder would receive a payment from the option writer as a cash settlement for the net profit.

Therefore a company that has tendered a price for a contract in a foreign currency might use currency options. A put option to sell the currency could be exercised in the event that it wins the contract and earns the currency, but allowed to lapse otherwise. However, covering tender-to-contract risk with currency options would make sense only if the chances of winning looked good. Too many unsuccessful tenders, all covered by currency options, would result in high and wasted premium costs.

Example

A Dutch company has tendered for a contract priced in dollars. If it wins the contract, it will receive a payment of $2,200,000 in two months' time. The dollar receipts will be converted immediately into euros.

The current euro/dollar spot rate is €1 = $1.05. This is expected to fall in the next few months as the dollar strengthens in line with good prospects for the US economy and US interest rates. The company is concerned about recent volatility in the exchange rate, however, and is worried that the dollar could weaken and the exchange rate, against expectation, might rise substantially.

Therefore the company buys a put option on $2,200,000 against the euro, at a strike price of €1 = $1.10, with an expiry date in two months' time.

Analysis

By purchasing a dollar put option at a strike price of 1.10, the company has guaranteed itself a minimum income of €2,000,000 ($2,200,000 ÷ 1.10), less the cost of the premium, in the event that the contract is won and the dollars are received.

If the contract is not won, the option will be allowed to lapse at expiry, if the exchange rate is below 1.10.

If the contract is not won, but the spot exchange rate rises above 1.10, the company can still exercise the option at 1.10, and the option writer might make a cash settlement for the net gain to the option holder.

For example, if the spot exchange rate at expiry is €1 = $1.12, the option would be settled for cash as follows

	€
Exercise option: holder sells $2,200,000 at 1.10	2,000,000.00
Spot transaction: holder buys $2,200,000 at 1.12	1,964,285.71
Net gain to the option holder, cash settlement	35,714.29

Instead of buying an option, the company could have sold $2 million two months forward, using a forward exchange contract. If the contract had not been won, the company would have been exposed to a large rise in the exchange rate, i.e. a strengthening dollar, and would have had to close out the forward contract by purchasing $2 million, i.e. buy dollars to sell them.

Uncertain Amounts of Currency

A problem also occurs with forward exchange contracts when the future amount of foreign currency income or expenditure is uncertain. Arranging forward contracts, i.e. binding contracts to buy or sell currency, could in those circumstances create currency exposures rather than hedge them, in much the same way as if the foreign currency receipt or payment didn't occur. For example, if a company expects to receive about $400,000 in six months, but is not certain of the exact amount, it might arrange a forward contract to sell $400,000. However, there will be a currency exposure for the amount by which actual receipts exceed or fall short of the $400,000. Currency options could be used to hedge the exposure for the uncertain amount of currency income or spending.

Example
An exporter earning regular income in dollars might estimate that its

dollar income in three months' time will be at least $1 million and possibly as much as $1.25 million or more. Its policy might be to

- arrange three months' forward cover to sell $1 million
- purchase a three-month' dollar put option for $250,000
- deal with any other surplus or deficit in dollar income through spot transactions.

This method of using currency options can be particularly valuable for hedging uncertain currency exposures where companies issue overseas price lists in foreign currency, and can only estimate what their currency earnings will be.

Currency Speculation

Currency options, by limiting the downside risk for the purchaser to the cost of the premium, can be used to speculate on future exchange rate movements when there is no underlying trade transaction. The option holder could profit from favorable spot price movements.

For example, by purchasing a dollar call option for $50 million at £1 = $1.50 at a cost of £400,000, a UK company might hope to profit from a fall in the sterling/dollar exchange rate. If the rate fell to $1.40 the option would be exercised to buy $50 million at $1.50, costing £33.3 million. Then the $50 million could be sold spot at $1.40 to raise £35.7 million, giving a gross speculative profit of £2.4 million (£35.7m - £33.3m) and a net profit of £2 million after deducting the cost of the premium.

The fact that only the premium is payable provides an opportunity for a high degree of *leverage* between the money at risk and the possible benefits. Here, the dealer would have gambled £400,000 and won £2.4 million. Premiums can be costly, however, and someone speculating on currency options could end up with embarrassing, if not excessive, losses purely from premium payments.

Credit-constrained Companies

A company that is credit-constrained because it is at or near its bank credit limits, may choose option cover for its currency exposures because options do not utilize the company's credit lines with the banks at all, unlike outright transactions in the forward market. This is because the bank bears no counterparty credit risk with an option holder because any settlement payment on exercise will be one-way, i.e. from the bank as option writer to the option holder.

5

Strike Prices

For over-the-counter options, the strike price or exercise price is chosen by the customer buying the option. Customers can stipulate whatever strike price they wish, but the bank will charge a higher or lower premium accordingly. For traded options, the available strike prices are decided by the options exchange, but several strike prices, typically seven, will be available for any given expiry date. The market price of options for the same expiry date will differ according to their strike price.

ATM, ITM and OTM Strike Prices

The strike price for a currency option might be equal to the exchange rate when the option is written, but also it might be above the current exchange rate or below it. Option strike prices fall into four categories

- in-the-money (ITM)
- out-of-the-money (OTM)
- at-the-money-spot (ATMS)
- at-the-money-forward (ATMF).

It is quite common for an option to be called at-the-money when its strike price equals the current spot rate of exchange. However, this is not strictly correct, and a distinction should be made between American-style and European-style options.

- An American-style option is at-the-money when its strike price equals the current spot exchange rate, when the delta of the option is near or exactly 50%. (Delta is explained in Chapter 6.)

- A European-style option is at-the-money when its strike price equals the forward rate for an outright forward exchange contract maturing on the option's expiry date, when its delta is about 50%.

An American-style option might be written at-the-money-spot (ATMS) and a European-style option might be written at-the-money-forward (ATMF).

An option is in-the-money when its strike price is more favorable to the option holder than an at-the-money strike price.

An in-the-money strike price for an American-style option is therefore more advantageous to the option holder than the current spot rate in the foreign exchange cash market. For example, if a company is looking to buy an American-style dollar put option giving it the right to sell a quantity of dollars into sterling for expiry one year hence and the current spot rate is $1.6250, then any strike rate below $1.6250 would be in-the-money. If the strike price is $.6100 the option would be in-the-money by 1.5 cents (per £1). When an option is in-the-money on expiry, it will be exercised, to give the option holder a profit.

A European-style option is in-the-money if its strike price is more favorable to the option holder than the exchange rate available for an outright forward contract maturing on the option's expiry date. It is in-the-money *at expiry* if its strike price is more favorable to the option holder than the current spot rate, and the option therefore will be exercised.

An option is out-of-the-money when its strike price is less favorable to the option holder than an at-the-money strike price.

An out-of-the-money strike price for an American-style option is therefore one that is less advantageous than the current spot rate. In the above example of an American-style dollar put option against sterling, any strike price above $1.6250 would be out-of-the-money. Unless the spot price moves above the strike price before the option's expiry date, the option holder will allow it to lapse.

A European-style option is out-of-the-money if its strike price is less favorable to the option holder than the rate available for an outright forward exchange contract maturing on the option's expiry/exercise date. It is out-of-the-money *at expiry* if its strike price is less favorable than the current spot rate, and the option will not be exercised.

Example
A company wishes to buy a European-style dollar put option giving it the right to sell dollars for sterling one year hence. The spot exchange rate is $1.6250. The forward points for a one-year forward contract are $0.0750 and the interest rate on dollars is lower than the interest rate on sterling.

Analysis
The forward points should be deducted because the interest rate is lower on dollars than sterling, and the dollar therefore is worth more forward against sterling than spot. The exchange rate for a forward contract would be $1.5500 (1.6250-0.0750). A European-style option at this strike price of $1.5500 would be at-the-money (ATMF). The ATMF strike price of $1.5500 differs from the spot rate of $1.6250 by $0.0750, the forward adjustment (forward points), and in this example for a dollar put option the forward price is more favorable than the spot rate.

This analysis of in-the-money, out-of-the-money and at-the-money applies to the strike price on the date the options are written. Because spot rates and forward rates change continually over time, options can change from being in-the-money to at-the-money, or out-of-the-money. If they start at-the-money, they are most likely to become in-the-money or out-of-the-money by the time the options reach their expiry/exercise date.

The examples reproduced might help to illustrate how a European-style call or put option can change from being in-the-money to out-of-the-money or vice versa in the period to expiry. These changes depend on changes in the forward rate, and whether the option is in-the-money, out-of-the-money or at-the-money when written. As the option approaches its expiry date, the forward rate should get closer in value to the spot rate. At expiry, the forward rate is the current spot rate.

Note that in the diagram, an option's strike price can be either in-the-money or out-of-the-money when it is higher than the current forward rate. This depends on how the exchange rate is quoted, i.e. which currency is the base currency and which is the variable or quoted currency.

Strike Prices: European-style Call Option (Dollar Call Against Sterling)

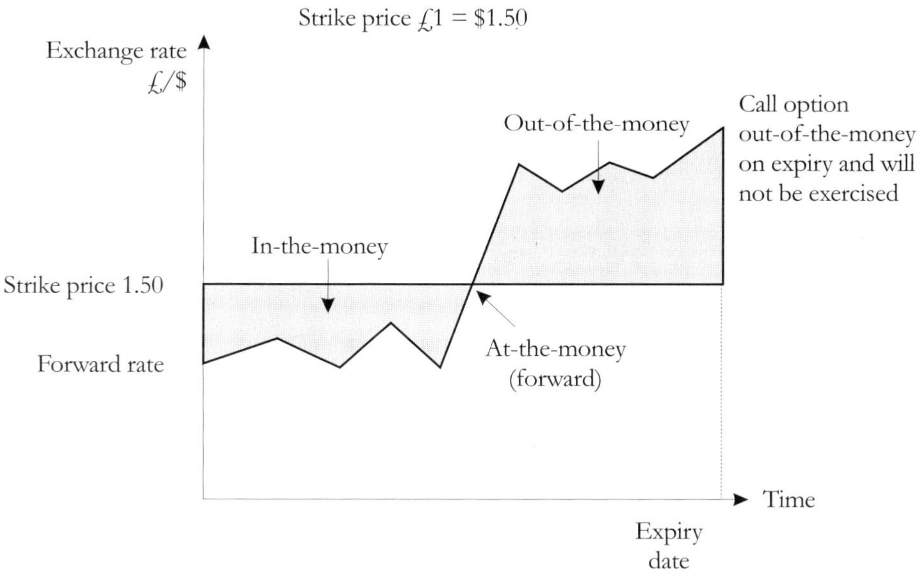

Strike Prices: European-style Put Option
(Dollar Put Against Sterling)

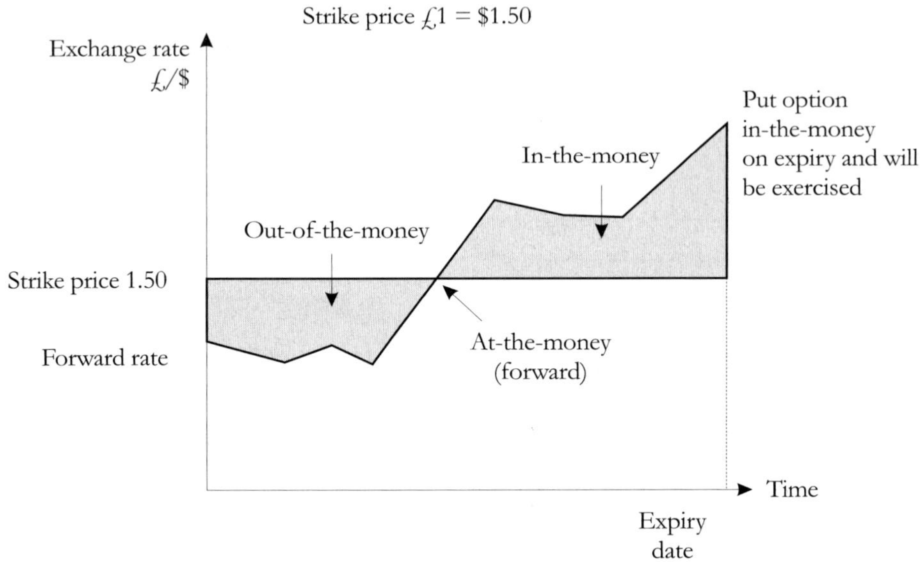

Note: at expiry, the "forward rate" = current spot rate

Strike Prices: European-style Call Option
(Dollar call against Swiss Franc)

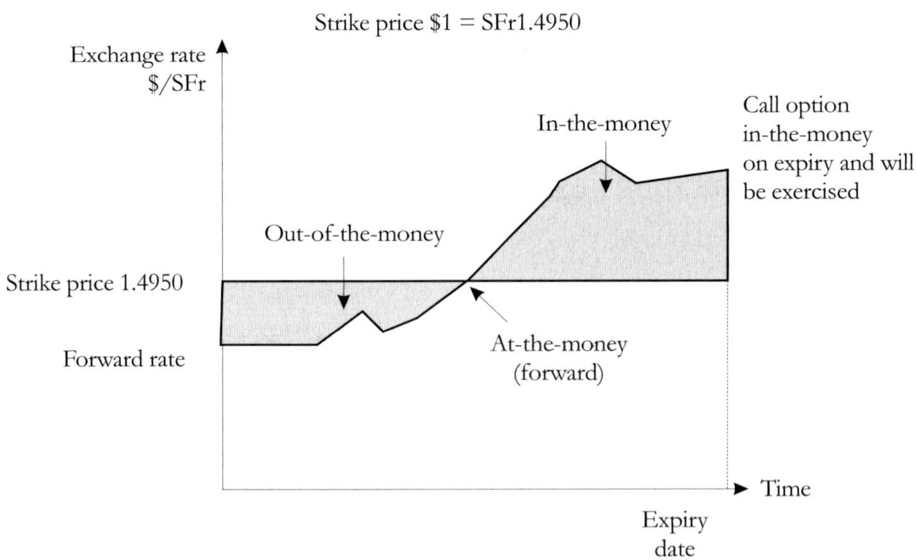

Strike Prices: European-style Call Option
(Dollar call against Swiss Franc)

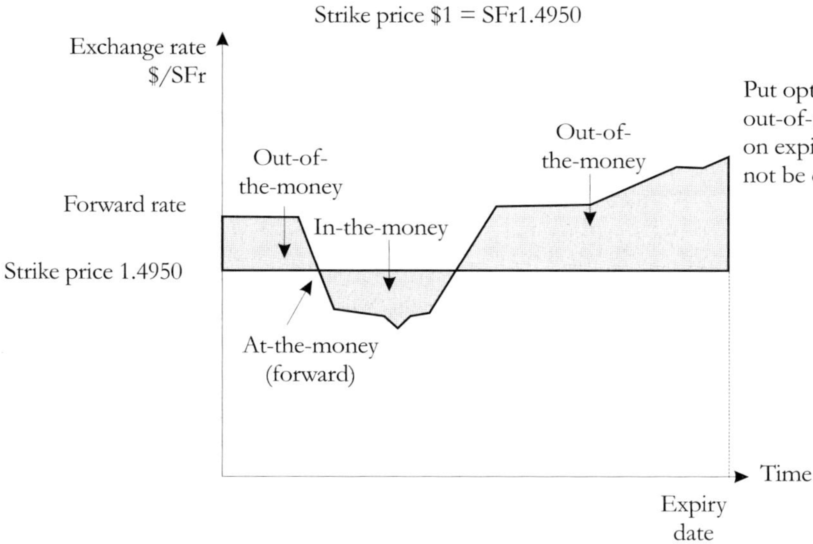

Note: at expiry, the "forward rate" = current spot rate

Example
On February 1, the euro/dollar spot rate is € = $1.0500-1.0510 and the three months' forward adjustment is 0.84-0.89 cents.

A company wishes to purchase a put option on $500,000 for expiry on May 1 from its bank and is considering each of several possible strike prices.

Analysis
A strike rate of $1.0510 would be at-the-money (ATMS) for an American-style option. A strike rate of $1.0599 (1.0510 + 0.0089) would be at-the money (ATMF) for a European-style option. The forward points are added in this case.

- A strike rate of $1.0450 would be 0.60 cents in-the-money for an American option and 1.49 cents in-the-money for a European option.

- A strike rate of $1.0600 would be 0.90 cents out-of-the-money for an American option and just 0.01 cents out-of-the-money for a European option.

Suppose that the company chooses to buy an American-style put option at $1.0600, for expiry on or before May 1.

- The spot rate on February 15 might have changed to $1.0480 and the option would now be even further out-of-the-money (1.20 cents).
- If the spot rate on March 1 were $1.0535, the option would be still out-of-the-money, but only by 0.65 cents.
- If the spot rate on April 12 were $1.0625, the option would have become in-the-money by 0.25 cents.
- If the spot rate on May 1 were $1.0750, it would be in-the-money by 1.5 cents and would be exercised, and the company would choose to sell $500,000 at the option price of $1.0600.

The significance of an ATMF strike price (European-style option) relates to a situation in which a company wishes to ensure that its worst possible exchange rate for a future purchase or sale of currency is as good as the exchange rate it could have obtained with a forward exchange contract.

Example

A UK company expects to receive $540,000 in three months' time that it will convert into sterling. The current spot rate of exchange is $1.5200 and the three months' forward rate is $1.5000.

Analysis

The company might decide to buy a European-style put option to sell the dollars with an expiry date in three months, instead of arranging a forward exchange contract. If it also wished to ensure that the exchange rate it eventually obtains for selling the dollars is no worse than the available forward rate, it would ask for a strike price of $1.5000. This is the at-the-money-forward strike price.

- If on expiry the spot rate is above $1.50, the company will exercise the option and sell the dollars in exchange for £360,000 ($540,000 ÷ 1.50).

- If on expiry the spot exchange rate were below $1.50, the company would let the option lapse and sell dollars at the spot rate, to earn in excess of £360,000. For example, if the spot rate were $1.45, the dollars could be sold for £372,414, over £12,414 more.

Ignoring the cost of the premium, the company therefore will do no worse and might do better than arranging a forward contract.

Relevance of the Strike Price to Potential Gains and Risk

The upside potential of an option will depend on whether the strike price is at-the-money, in-the-money, or out-of-the-money when it is written. An option holder will profit from the purchase of the option if the strike price is more favorable than the spot rate when the option expires, and the option is exercised, provided that the gain from the difference between the strike price and the spot rate exceeds the cost of the option premium. The risk to the option holder is that the option will be worthless on expiry date and will not be exercised, so that there is a loss of the premium paid.

The option premium will vary with the strike price relative to current spot market rates or forward rates when the option is written.

- If the strike price were in-the-money when the option was written, it is likely to be in-the-money at expiry date. The risk that the option will not be exercised therefore is relatively small. As a consequence, the premium will be relatively high to compensate the option writer.
- For an option with a significantly out-of-the-money strike rate, the option premium will be low because the exchange rate will have to move a long way before the option is worth exercising.

Example

A company wishes to purchase $400,000 in exchange for sterling in six months' time. The spot rate is $1.4500 and the six months' forward rate is $1.4250. The company is considering using a European-style option to hedge this dollar exposure.

Another course of action being considered is to do nothing, and buy $400,000 at whatever spot rate is prevailing in six months' time.

The premium for an option would depend on the strike price, and three prices are under consideration

	Strike price	**Premium**
At-the-money-spot (ATMS)	$1.4500	2.5 pence per dollar
At-the-money-forward (ATMF)	$1.4250	1.5 pence per dollar
Out-of-the-money	$1.4000	0.5 pence per dollar

Analysis

For an ATMS strike price, the premium would be £10,000. Buying an option at this price would result in the same overall cost for the company, compared with the alternative of waiting for six months and buying $400,000 at the then spot rate, if the spot rate in six months' time is as follows

	£
Premium for option	10,000
Cost of buying $400,000 at strike price of $1.45	275,862
Breakeven cost	285,862

The breakeven spot rate is £1 = $1.3993 ($400,000 ÷ £285,862). Unless the spot rate is below this on expiry date, the option holder will have made a loss on his option purchase because it would have been cheaper to do nothing for six months and then buy dollars at the spot rate. The spot exchange rate would have to fall in the six-month period to expiry by over five cents from its current level of $1.4500 for the decision to buy the option to show a profit.

At an ATMF strike price of $1.4250, the premium would be £6,000.

Compared with a decision not to hedge the exposure, wait for six months and then buy $400,000 spot, the breakeven spot rate on expiry date would be as follows

	£
Premium for option	6,000
Cost of buying $400,000 at strike price of 1.4250	280,702
Breakeven cost	286,702

This gives a breakeven spot rate of £1 = $1.3952 ($400,000 ÷ £286,702). Unless the spot price is $1.3952 or lower in six months, the call option holder would make a loss because it would have been cheaper to do nothing for six months and then buy dollars at the spot rate. For the company to make a profit in this situation from buying a call option, the spot price would have to move in the six-month period from its current level of $1.4500 to below $1.3952, a change of about 5.5 cents.

At an out-of-the-money strike price of $1.4000, the premium would be £2,000 and the option would be out-of-the-money by five cents when written. Again, comparing the use of an option with a decision to wait for six months and then buy $400,000 spot, the breakeven spot rate on expiry date would have to be

	£
Premium for option	2,000
Cost of buying $400,000 at strike price of 1.4000	285,714
Breakeven cost	287,714

This gives a breakeven spot rate of £1 = $1.3903 ($400,000 ÷ £287,714), and the spot price would have to be less than this after six months, a movement of about six cents from the current spot rate for the option holder to make a profit. Otherwise it would be cheaper to do nothing, wait for six months and then buy the dollars spot.

Because the premium will be lower for a strike price that is further out-of-the-money, and higher for a strike price that is further in-the-money, the maximum loss for the option holder varies according to the strike price.

Because of the premium, in the period between the creation of the option and its expiry, the spot price might have to move by a smaller amount for an out-of-the-money option than for an at-the-money option, before the breakeven point is reached and buying an option becomes profitable. The spot rate might have to move by an even larger amount before an in-the-money option became profitable for its holder.

Strike Prices and Option Premiums

An option that is in-the-money when it is written will cost more to buy than an at-the-money option, and more still than an out-of-the-money option. The cost of an option will depend on the extent to which it is in-the-money or out-of-the-money when written.

- The lower the value of the underlying currency at the option's strike price relative to the spot price or forward price, the more valuable a call option will be.
- The higher the value of the underlying currency at the option's strike price relative to the spot price or forward price, the more valuable a put option will be.

Example
A bank writes four currency options simultaneously. Each option is a European-style put or call option on dollars, with expiry in three months' time.

Put/call	Currency	Amount	Other currency	Strike price
				€/$
Call	dollars	$1,000,000	euros	€ = $1.05
Put	dollars	$1,000,000	euros	€ = $1.05
Call	dollars	$1,000,000	euros	€ = $1.08
Put	dollars	$1,000,000	euros	€ = $1.08

Analysis
The two call options are identical except for their strike price. At the

strike price for each option, the value of the $1,000,000, the underlying currency, is €952,380.95 and €925,925.92 for strike prices of 1.05 and 1.08 respectively. The call option with the lower value, €925,925.92 (strike price 1.08), will be worth more than the option with the higher value, €952,380.95 (strike price 1.05).

On the other hand, for the put options written at the same strike prices of 1.05 and 1.08, the option with the 1.05 strike price will cost more than the option with the 1.08 strike price.

A price information screen for traded options is illustrated. This shows the indicative cost of a premium, for Swiss franc call and put options against dollars, for expiry in the months of March and June. The strike price is expressed in cents per Swiss franc, rather than SFr per dollar. Each option contract is a put or call on SFr62,500.

Notice how a call option costs less when the value of the underlying currency at the strike price is higher. For example, taking the illustrative figures in the table, a March call option at a strike price of 65 cents (value $40,625 or 62,500 x $0.65) costs 3.06 cents per SFr, whereas a similar option at a higher strike price of 71 cents (value $44,375 or 62,500 x $0.71) costs just 0.09 cents per SFr.

For similar reasons, a put option costs less when the value of the underlying currency at the strike price is lower.

Strike Prices and Premiums

Swiss franc options against dollars SFr62,500 per contract. Premiums shown in cents per SFr

Current Spot Price (cents per SFr)	Strike Price (cents per SFr)	Calls		Puts	
SFr		Mar	Jun	Mar	Jun
68.14	65	3.06	3.24	0.10	0.21
68.14	66	2.18	2.62	0.23	1.30
68.14	67	1.21	1.77	0.41	1.66
68.14	68	0.57	1.10	0.70	1.87
68.14	69	0.34	0.94	1.37	2.74
68.14	70	0.22	0.87	2.46	4.02
68.14	71	0.09	0.68	3.32	4.73

6

Option Premiums

For over-the-counter options, the terms of the option, including premiums, are negotiated between the purchaser and the option writer. The bank writing the option will specify what premium it will require for an option with given terms, but the customer can negotiate a lower premium by agreeing to a different strike price, or by agreeing to a European rather than an American-style option, etc. For exchange-traded options, premiums are the market prices at which they are purchased and sold.

The Amount of the Premium

The amount of premium depends on several factors

- the exchange rate (strike price) specified in the option and whether this is above, below, or equal to the current rate
- the tenor of the option, or the period of time to the expiry date
- the expected volatility of the exchange rate between the two currencies
- interest rates for the two currencies
- whether the option can be exercised at any time up to expiry (American) or at expiry date only (European).

Banks will seek to make a profit on their options trading, and the size of a bank's spread, the difference between the price at which it will sell a call option and a comparable put option, also will affect the price.

Mathematical models are used by banks to calculate their options prices, or to assess prices being offered by other banks or in the exchange-traded market. These mathematical models, such as the Black-Scholes model, are based on an options pricing theory that seeks to establish how the various influences on option prices should work.

Option pricing theory assumes there are two components to the premium price, an intrinsic value and a time value. Premiums that are quoted should combine an element of each.

Currency Option Premium

Intrinsic Value	+	**Time Value**
Influences:		Influences:
Strike price		Time to expiry
Spot price or forward rate		Exchange rate volatility
		Domestic interest rate

Time value is the more complex component to estimate, although in practise it can be calculated as the difference between the option premium and the option's intrinsic value.

Intrinsic Value

The intrinsic value of an option on the spot currency is the difference between its strike price and the current spot rate of exchange (American-style option) or forward rate of exchange (European-style option).

Strike Price Compared with Current Spot Price (American-style Options) or Forward Rate (European-style Options)

	Name given to option	**Intrinsic value**
Same	At-the-money	Nil
Less favorable	Out-of-the-money	Negative – the underlying exchange rate has to move up to the strike rate merely to take the intrinsic value to nil
More favorable	In-the-money	Positive – difference between strike price and the spot rate (American options) or forward rate (European options)

Example

Suppose that the strike price for an American-style sterling/dollar option is $1.50. If the current spot rate is $1.50, and the option is at-the-money, the price of the option has no intrinsic value, and the premium will consist entirely of time value.

If the strike price for an American-style call option on dollars against sterling is $1.50 and the spot rate is $1.54, the option is out-of-the-money because it would be cheaper to buy dollars at the spot rate of $1.54. The intrinsic value of the option is minus $0.04. While market prices cannot be negative, the impact of intrinsic value on the option-pricing equation (option-pricing model) can be negative because the negative intrinsic value can be set against the time-value element of the option to obtain a premium that is lower than the option's time value.

If the strike price for an American-style call option on dollars against sterling is $1.50 and the spot rate is $1.47, the option is in-the-money, and has an intrinsic value of $0.03 simply because it would be cheaper by this amount to buy dollars at the strike price than at the spot rate.

Time Value

The time value of an option exists for the reasons that make it worth buying an option now that might or might not be exercised at a time in the future. Time value arises from the degree of probability that the underlying market price, the rate of exchange in the case of currency options, could move sufficiently in the option holder's favor in the period up to the option's maturity to create some profit for the option holder and a loss for the option writer.

Time to expiry

The longer the time period to expiry of the option, the greater will be the likelihood of exchange rate movements in the option holder's favor. The probability that the option will be exercised is greater and so the premium will be higher to compensate the option writer for the risk.

Suppose, for example, that a European dollar put option against yen has a strike price of $1 = ¥120, and the current spot rate is 122. Market expectations are that the yen will strengthen, perhaps to about 118, over the next few weeks or months. If the option's expiry date is in one week's time, the option will have some time value. However, if expiry is in two months, the option's time value will be higher because the likelihood of a movement in the exchange rate below the strike price of 120 will be greater.

The time value of an option should fall as it approaches expiry. The rate at which this value falls is known as time decay that is estimated mathematically in option pricing models. It becomes more rapid as an option gets closer to its expiry date because the likelihood of large exchange rate movements diminishes substantially.

Time Decay Curve

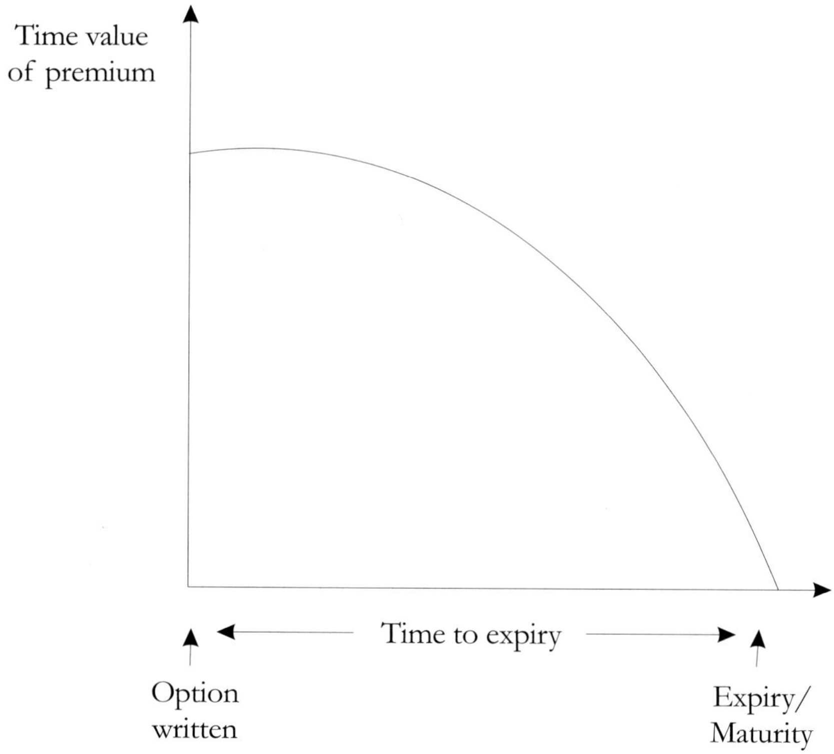

Volatility of Exchange Rates

The reason for buying currency options is uncertainty about future exchange rate movements. When exchange rate movements could be large, options will have a greater value than when rate movements are expected to be fairly small. Greater exchange rate volatility adds to an option's value.

Future volatility is uncertain, but can be assessed either by

- looking at the history of exchange rates between the currencies, and volatility in the past, or
- speculating/forecasting what volatility might be in the future, given economic and political conditions in the country of each currency.

Volatility is measured mathematically. Measuring volatility and the effect of volatility on option pricing is explained in further detail in the Appendix.

Domestic Interest Rates

The purchaser of an option must pay a premium up front, and there is an implied interest cost in paying out cash to buy an option instead of being able to invest it on deposit. The option writer, on the other hand, receives the premium and can invest the money up to the option's expiry/maturity.

The domestic interest rate, i.e. the interest rate in which the premium is paid, affects the option premium. The price of an option should be reduced to allow for the interest benefit to the option writer and the cost to the option buyer of the premium. If domestic interest rates rose by 1% per annum, the interest cost to a buyer of a six-month option whose premium previously would have been €1,000 would rise by €5 (1% of €1,000 x $^{6}/_{12}$). The value of the option to the buyer therefore will fall by this amount just as it will rise to the option writer (the bank), that can place the cash received on deposit to earn 1% per annum extra over the six-month period to expiry. Therefore we should expect the premium to fall in price by €5.

Deltas, Gammas, Thetas and Vegas

Dealers in options use a number of ratios for monitoring changes in option prices in response to changes in factors that affect their intrinsic value or time value.

Delta Values

Delta is a ratio that measures the change in an option's price in relation to a change in the spot rate of exchange.

$$\text{Delta} = \frac{\text{Change in option premium}}{\text{Change in currency spot rate}}$$

The value of an option's delta can be anything between zero and one, and it will not be constant at every spot rate. An option's delta will change as the spot rate changes.

- An option that is deeply in-the-money and with a short time to expiry will have little or no time value, and its price will consist almost entirely of intrinsic value. A change in the spot rate will alter intrinsic value by the same amount, and delta will be equal or close to one.
- An option that is deeply out-of-the-money has no intrinsic value and a change in the spot price is unlikely to affect the option's value significantly. Delta will be equal to or close to zero.
- An option that is at-the-money has a delta of about 0.5.

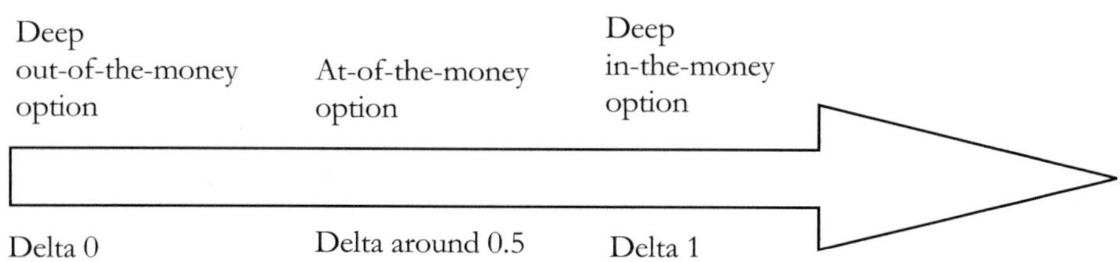

Delta values are useful for a number of reasons.

- Although the delta value for an option changes with the option's premium, it is a useful ready measure for estimating the likely change in premium if the spot exchange alters.
- Options traders might use a hedging method known as delta hedging. Companies that deal in options, e.g. banks, might choose to hedge their options position (exposures) by purchasing or selling currency in the spot markets. Delta hedging is a system for deciding how much to buy or sell.

Delta Hedging

Delta hedging is a system of trading rules that uses a mathematical model, based on the Black-Scholes option pricing model, to calculate the appropriate size of hedge that a writer of options should obtain to minimize the risks from his trading position. It is used primarily by banks to calculate the size of hedge that they need for their currency options trading positions.

The mathematics are beyond the scope of this book. However, it might be useful to see in broad terms how delta hedging works.

Suppose that a bank writes a European-style Swiss Franc call option for SFr10 million against the dollar at a strike price that is at-the-money-forward, $1 = SFr1.70. On the assumption of a 50-50 probability at this time that the option eventually will be exercised, the bank could hedge its position by purchasing 50% of the option's amount, in this example SFr5 million in exchange for dollars, at the current forward rate of SFr1.70.

The effect of hedging is to reduce the likelihood that the bank will make a loss on its options position. At the same time hedging reduces the bank's potential profit. This is because

- if the exchange rate moves in the option holder's favor, the bank's loss on its options position will be offset to some extent by the profit from having purchased the call currency at the forward rate, but
- if the exchange rate moves in the option writer's favor, there will be a loss on the purchase of the call currency at the forward rate.

In the example above, if the exchange rate at the option's expiry is SFr1.68, the position of the bank with a 50% delta hedge would be

	$	$
Bank's loss on option position		
Call value of SFr10 million at 1.70	5,882,353	
Spot value of SFr10 million at 1.68	5,952,381	
Loss to option writer		-70,028
Bank's gain on forward purchase		
Cost of SFr5 million at 1.70	2,941,176	
Current resale value of SFr5 million at 1.68	2,976,190	
Profit		+35,014
Net loss		-35,014

The delta hedge reduces the loss. The bank could expect that the option premium will be sufficient to cover the rest of the loss, leaving it with a net profit, or at worst break-even on its options position.

The dollar/Swiss franc forward exchange rate will change over the period to expiry of the option. For a call option, if the Swiss franc falls in value, it will become less likely that the option eventually will be exercised, and the bank can reduce the level of its hedge from 50% (SFr5 million) to a lower amount by selling Swiss francs for dollars.

On the other hand, if the Swiss franc increases in value, it will become more likely that the option eventually will be exercised, and the bank therefore should increase the size of its hedge by purchasing more Swiss francs.

As the option's expiry approaches, the size of the delta hedge will move towards 100% if the option is in-the-money, and towards 0% if the option is out-of-the-money.

The Option's Delta Value and Delta Hedging

The delta value of an option can be used to quantify the amount of Swiss francs to buy or sell to create a suitable hedge. If it becomes more likely that the option will be exercised, its delta value will rise, and if exercise becomes less probable, the delta value will fall.

Continuing the example, suppose that an increase in the value of the Swiss franc increases the delta value of the option from 0.50 to 0.60. The delta hedging system would determine that the bank should increase the size of its hedge to SFr6 million (SFr10 million x 0.60) by purchasing a further SFr1 million in the FX market, in order to regain delta neutrality.

The diagram summarizes the concept. The delta curve shows the delta value of a call option at different exchange rates, rising from zero to one, and the percentage of the option value that should be hedged by purchases of the currency. A similar delta hedging curve can be constructed for put options. Note that the hedge ratio for an at-the-money option is about 50%, because the delta of an at-the-money option is about 50%.

Delta Hedging: Call Options (At-the-money when written)

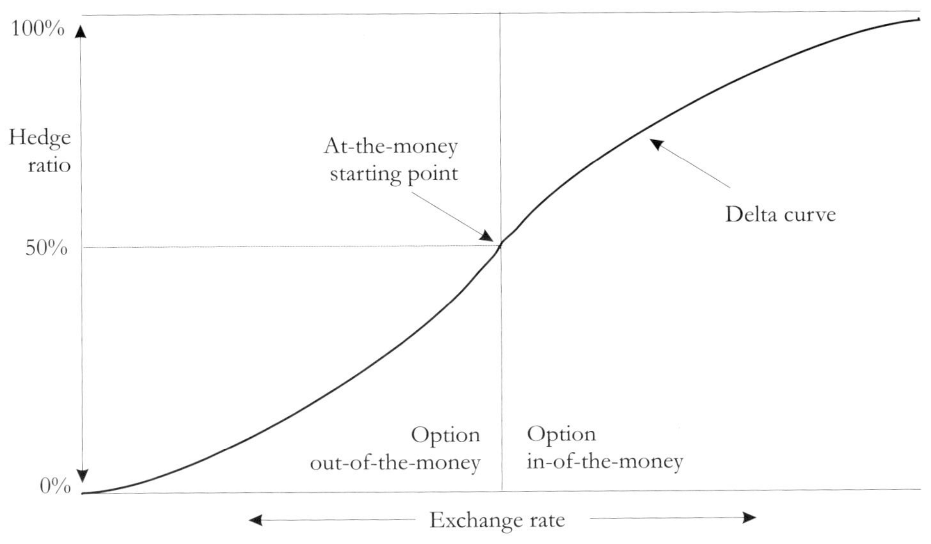

Gammas, Thetas and Vegas

Other options ratios used by dealers are gammas, thetas and vegas.

Gamma

A gamma ratio is the ratio of the percentage rate of change in delta to the percentage rate of change in the spot rate. For example, if an option has a gamma of 0.80 when its delta is 0.65 and the exchange rate is 1.50, a 1% increase in the exchange rate will increase or lower the delta, depending on whether the option is a call or a put, by 0.8% (0.80 x 1%), to 0.6552 or 0.6448. Actually, the delta will change by a slightly different amount because both delta and gamma values change as the asset price changes. An option's gamma is at its largest value when the option is at-the-money, and is zero for options that are deeply out-of-the-money, or deeply in-the-money, with deltas of 0 or 1.

Theta

A theta value measures the amount by which an option's value declines as time elapses. It can be measured as follows.

$$\text{Theta} = \frac{\text{\% change in option price}}{\text{\% change in time to expiry}}$$

Because the option price falls as the option approaches expiry, an option's theta is a higher value close to expiry and lower when there is a longer period to expiry.

Therefore a theta value is used as a measure of time decay, i.e. the rate of change in an option's premium as it approaches expiry.

Vega

A vega ratio measures the change in an option's premium relative to a change in the volatility of the exchange rate.

$$\text{Vega} = \frac{\text{\% change in value of option}}{\text{\% change in time to expiry}}$$

Vega (for plain vanilla options) always must be a positive value. If volatility increases, the value of an option (call or put) also will rise.

The vega ratio can be useful for monitoring the significance of exchange rate volatility on option premiums.

Summary

An option premium is the sum of its intrinsic value and its time value.

- When an option is out-of-the-money, there is less prospect of the option being exercised or having value to the buyer because it would need a greater exchange rate movement to bring it in-the-money. The negative intrinsic value affects the option's time value. Time value falls as the strike price moves further out-of-the-money.
- The further an option is in-the-money, the more its intrinsic value will determine its price. The time to expiry and uncertainty of future exchange rate movements become a smaller influence.

Volatility in the underlying exchange rate is a significant influence on time value. A mathematical measure of volatility can be obtained from historical exchange rate data.

Over-the-counter Options

OTC options are sold by individual banks to their customers and are tailor-made to the customer's requirements. Large companies might use them extensively, depending on the preferences of the finance director or corporate treasurer for options over spot market transactions and forward exchange contracts. Small and medium-sized companies face the difficulty that although their bank will be willing in principle to sell OTC options to them, the quality of service is likely to vary within the branch network.

Buying an OTC Option

An OTC option is arranged through a bank. Companies seeking to buy an option should first determine the details of the option required

- amount of currency
- put or call option
- expiry date or exercise period
- the strike price required
- whether the option should be on the spot or the forward currency.

A bank will be prepared to write an option for any convertible currencies and for a specific expiry date to suit the option buyer. The exercise period for an OTC option (the time to expiry) can be longer than for exchange-traded options, but this is an item for negotiation between the bank and the customer because the bank might wish to charge a large premium for long-term options.

Once arranged, the terms of the option are not subject to amendment. The option holder cannot sell the option on to a third party because the agreement is exclusively between the original buyer and the bank. He might be able to redeem it before expiry, but only at the bank that wrote the option. In such circumstances, the redemption value of the option would be for the bank to decide, and the option might be worthless in the bank's judgment.

Smaller companies wishing to buy an option should approach their local bank, specifying details such as the currencies involved, strike price, expiry date, etc. The branch might make some suggestions for change such as pointing out the higher premium cost for more favorable strike rates, and then phoning one of the bank's foreign exchange dealing rooms. A premium will be quoted by the dealing room and relayed to the company that must accept or reject the price.

If accepted, the company will be asked to confirm its request in writing or by fax, and to pay the premium. In some cases, a written request is necessary *before* a premium is quoted. The bank will confirm the option details on the same day by fax.

Large companies with direct phone access to banks' foreign exchange dealing rooms can arrange option details and the premium for an option without the intermediation of the local branch. For a given strike rate, a bank will quote bid and offer prices for put and call options respectively, and the company doesn't have to indicate in advance whether it wants to buy a put or a call option.

Option Writing by Corporate Treasuries

In some large companies, a central treasury department is set up as a profit center to provide banking services to the rest of the group. This might include writing OTC options for a subsidiary, instead of buying them from banks or an options exchange.

The subsidiary company buying the option from the central treasury department obtains the hedge it wants against the risk exposure. And just as a bank takes on the customer's risk when it writes an option, so too will the group's central treasury assume the subsidiary's risk. The treasury department, as a quasi bank, must decide if and how it is going to hedge its own exposures, perhaps by buying suitable hedging instruments itself from banks such as options, futures, forward exchange contracts, etc.

Conclusion

Banks now sell OTC options to customers more actively than in the past, but options are not as widely used by companies as forward exchange contracts, nor are they likely to be worthwhile for small companies trading in small amounts of foreign currency.

8

Exchange-traded Options

Traded currency options are written, bought and sold on a number of options exchanges around the world. In contrast to OTC options, there is a physical market for traded options. Exchange authorities set options specifications and regulate trading activities. Traded currency options are standardized contracts for specified amounts of one currency against another and with specified expiry dates. Strike prices at which options can be traded also are specified by the exchange authorities.

The Philadelphia Stock Exchange

The Philadelphia Stock Exchange (PHLX) is the largest market for traded currency options. The German DTB, now part of Eurex, trades a $/DM option and there is a currency options market in Amsterdam. Montreal and Sydney that used to trade FX options, no longer do so. The Chicago Mercantile Exchange (IMM division) trades options on currency futures.

Note:
The Philadelphia Stock Exchange's trading hours are 2.30am USET to 2.30pm USET.

The PHLX currently lists 10 standardized currency options. Eight of these are for exchange rates against the dollar, and most options are available in either European or American style.

Of the 10 listed currency options, four involve legacy currencies: i.e. currencies that are in the process of disappearing because of EMU (dollar/Fr, dollar/deutschemark, deutschemark/yen and sterling/deutschemark). In addition around 110 FX pairs are traded on United Currency Options Market (UCOM).

The PHLX currency option specifications, for regular options, are

Against the dollar

Currency	Ticker symbol American	European	Contract	Premium
Sterling	XBP	CBP	£31,250	Cents per unit
Australian dollars	XAD	CAD	A$50,000	Cents per unit
Canadian dollars	XCD	CCD	C$50,000	Cents per unit
Deutschemarks	XDM	CDM	DM62,500	Cents per unit
French francs	XFF	CFF	F250,000	Tenths of a cent per unit
Yen	XJY	CJY	¥6,250,000	Hundredths of a cent per unit
Swiss francs	XSF	CSF	SFr62,500	Cents per unit
Euro	XEU	ECU	€62,500	Cents per unit

Cross-Rate options

Deutschemarks/Yen	-	MYX	DM62,500	In yen
Sterling/Deutschemarks	-	PMX	£31,250	In DM
Sterling/Yen	-	PIX	£31,250	In yen

Cross-rate options are for exchange rates not involving the dollar and are settled in a currency other than the dollar. These were introduced by PHLX in 1991.

PHLX also trades customized, as opposed to standardized, VEX options. Customized options give the customer a large say in deciding the specifications of the contract.

Customized options were introduced as a response to declining volumes of trade on PHLX.

Trading on PHLX

A traded options market has three types of participant

- specialists
- market-makers
- floor brokers.

All these participants are members of PHLX.

Specialists write a particular type of option. There is one specialist per currency option. The role of the specialist is always to provide a buy and a sell price. In addition he/she maintains an orderly market in the options, and looks after public orders that are not operable at current prices.

Market-makers buy and sell options secondhand to create a market, trading for their own account. Market-makers must be members of the exchange.

Floor brokers execute business on behalf of customers. Major banks offer such a broking service to non-bank customers, and there also are specialist broking firms.

Once it has opened an account with a broker, a company can buy or sell options by phone. The price of the premium obtained by the broker will be reported back to the company by phone, and details of the trade will be confirmed by fax. Typically, confirmations go out as soon as the floor trader is able to do so after executing the trade.

Premiums must be paid immediately from the company's client account, and a broker firm will refuse the trade unless sufficient funds are in the account. The company also will have to pay the broker a commission for its services, the amount depending on the size and frequency of trades with the broker, i.e. on the dealing relationship.

Features of Traded Options

Traded options are similar in most respects to OTC options, but do have special features. They are available only for major currencies, mainly for one currency against the dollar. Each option is for a *standard amount of currency*.

If, for example, a bank or company wishes to purchase PHLX put options on SFr6,250,000 into dollars, it would have to buy 100 options of SFr62,500 each.

A traded option contract can be defined by five elements

- type (put or call)
- style (American or European)
- underlying currencies, e.g. yen against the dollar
- strike price
- expiry date.

Within an exchange all traded options that are of the same type, style, and underlying currencies are referred to as a *class* of options. For example, European call options on Swiss francs into dollars are a class of options. Options in the same class that also have the same strike price and expiration date are referred to as a *series* of options. For example, all June 2000 American put options on sterling into dollars at a strike price of $1.60 make up a series of options.

American and European-traded Options

Options exchanges trade in both American and European-style options. On the Philadelphia Exchange, there are American and European options for every currency against the dollar. Cross-rate options on the PHLX are available in European-style only.

Although European options can be exercised only on expiry date, they can be bought and re-sold during their tenor, i.e. before expiry.

- They do not have to be purchased at the time of introduction of a new series of options. Options in the series can be bought at any time up to expiry.
- They can be sold at any time before expiry at their market value.

Considerable flexibility can be obtained from being able to open and close positions by buying and selling at times to suit the option user. The Philadelphia Stock Exchange's own publicity material has made this point strongly.

Most options are not exercised. For the most part they are closed out (sold or repurchased) prior to expiration. This fact is extremely important in assessing the usefulness of currency options. In a foreign currency market replete with uncertainty, it is comforting to realize that exchange-traded options are designed to be established or terminated as the need or desire arises.

The existence of a liquid and continuously active secondary market in trade currency options is crucial to providing option users with this level of flexibility.

Expiry Months and Dates

Regular traded options have standard expiry dates up to 12 months ahead. Typically the expiry months for standardized options are

- March
- June
- September
- December
- plus up to two additional near-term months.

This gives a quarterly expiry cycle with up to two near-term months that are months between now and the next quarterly expiry month.

For example, in early January options will be traded with expiry dates of January, February, March, June, September and December. In late January, after the January series has expired, there will be trading in options with expiry dates of February, March, June, September and December.

Within each expiry month, there is

- an expiry date that is the last day for exercising the options

- an expiry settlement date, when payments or the exchange of currencies take place.

On the Philadelphia Exchange, the expiry settlement date is the third Wednesday in the expiry month, and expiry date is the preceding Saturday, in effect this is the close of trading on the Friday before settlement date.

In addition to regular options, PHLX also trades month-end options, and long-term options, 13 to 24 months and 25 to 36 months, for some currencies.

Customized options can expire on any business day up to two years out.

Integrity of Traded Option Contracts

A liquid market in options can be maintained only if every buyer has complete faith that the option writer will fulfill his/her contract obligations if the option is exercised. The integrity of traded options is provided by the stock exchange.

On PHLX, all currency options are guaranteed by the exchange's clearing house, the Options Clearing Corporation (OCC). The OCC is jointly owned by PHLX, the American Stock Exchange (Amex), the Chicago Board Options Exchange (CBOE) and the Pacific Exchange (PCX). The OCC acts as the other side of each completed transaction.

- If an option holder exercises an option, he will notify the OCC through his broker, and will look to the OCC for the option writer's obligations to be fulfilled.
- The OCC in turn will randomly select option writers to meet the writer's obligations when an option is exercised.

The OCC protects its own financial position in various ways.

- It imposes strict financial standards for its clearing members. All options transactions on the exchange are processed through a clearing member firm.
- Option buyers must pay the premium up-front. The option

buyer's broker then pays premiums to the OCC.

- Option writers must pay a margin via their broker to the OCC, as a good faith deposit. If the option writer incurs a loss on his position, the OCC can ask for supplementary margin payments. The effect of margin payments is to cover losses that the option writer might incur, and ensure that funds will be available to pay the option holder should the option be exercised.
- The OCC also maintains a Clearing Fund, provided by contributions from clearing members. The fund is available to meet the obligations to option holders in the event that option writers default on their obligations and margins are insufficient to cover the payments to the option holders.

Settlement

The settlement of a traded option is organized by the clearing house for the exchange. On the PHLX, settlement is organized by the OCC. When an option is exercised by notification to the customer's broker, the option holder or writer must, depending on the terms of the option agreement

- deliver dollars into a bank account of the OCC in the US, receiving another currency in exchange, or
- deliver foreign currency into a bank account of the OCC in the country of the currency's origin, receiving dollars in exchange, except in the case of cross-currency options.

The OCC has a bank account in the country of each of the currencies for which it trades options.

The OCC will arrange for the exchange of currencies with the option holder.

Closing Out a Position

Most option positions are closed out before expiry. An option holder can sell an option, making a profit or loss on the difference between the original purchase price and the selling price.

For example, suppose that a company buys 50 June Swiss franc calls with an exercise price of 60, i.e. 60 cents per SFr, at a premium of 4.5 cents, and later sells 50 June SFr calls at the same exercise price to close the position. If the sale price of the SFr calls was 6 cents, there will be a profit of 1.5 cents per SFr (6 - 4.5) on the transactions.

	$
Purchase cost (50 contracts x SFr62,500 x 4.5 cents)	140,625
Sale price (50 contracts x SFr62,500 x 6 cents)	187,500
Profit	46,875

Because the options position has been closed out before expiry, there cannot be any exercise/settlement of the options when the expiry date is reached.

Exercise Prices

Exercise prices and premiums for traded options are quoted in an amount of one currency per unit of the other. On the Philadelphia Exchange this is normally in dollars and cents per unit of the other currency.

Examples
An exercise price of $0.60 for a call option on Swiss francs against dollars gives its holder the right to buy SFr62,500, the amount of the option, for $37,500 (62,500 x $0.60).

An exercise price of $1.55 for a put option for sterling into dollars gives its holder the right to sell £31,250, the amount of the option, in exchange for $48,437.50 (31,250 x $1.55).

Exercise prices for standard options are set at standard intervals by exchange authorities. For example, on the PHLX.

Option	Exercise price interval Three nearest months	6, 9 and 12 months	Over 12 months
Australian dollar	1 cent	1 cent	N/A
Sterling	1 cent	2 cents	4 cents
Canadian dollar	0.5 cents	0.5 cents	N/A
Euro	2 cents	2 cents	N/A

When trading is introduced in options with a new expiry month, the exchange sets the exercise prices. These prices will reflect the current spot rate of exchange, and in general

- at least four options will have an exercise price above the current spot rate, and
- four options will have an exercise price below the spot rate.

As the spot price changes over time, the exchange might introduce additional options with the same expiry month, but with a higher or lower exercise price.

For customized options, there is greater flexibility in the selection of the exercise price.

Premiums (Market Prices)

The premiums for exchange-traded options are the prices that bring buyers and sellers together, and so reflect supply and demand. However, it is generally recognized that the premium on a traded option at any time represents the market consensus of what the option is worth. This value is said to consist of intrinsic value and time value.

- The cost of options at a more distant exercise date will be higher because there is more time for exchange rates to change, giving better prospects for profiting on exercising the options, i.e. a higher time value.
- Taken together, the strike price plus the cost of the premium for the option will be less favorable than the available rate on a forward contract. For example, if a company could arrange a three months'

forward contract to sell dollars in exchange for sterling at £1 = $1.50, a traded call option at a strike price of $1.475 would have a premium cost higher than $0.025 per £1, perhaps six cents ($0.06) per pound sterling, to make the effective exchange rate obtainable from the option in excess of $1.50.

Price Information

Information about current market prices (premiums) are available to dealers and their clients on screen-based information systems such as Reuters and Bloomberg. Some information also is published in the daily financial press, giving close-of-trade prices for the previous day. An example of published prices for sterling options on the Philadelphia Stock Exchange is shown below.

- Premiums are quoted in units of one currency per unit of the other. On the PHLX, premiums are quoted mostly in cents per unit of the other currency.
- If the premium on a particular Swiss franc option is 2.54, this is 2.54 cents per Swiss franc. Because the Swiss franc option is for SFr62,500, the cost of purchasing one option would be $1,587.75 (62,500 x 2.54 cents). Similarly, the premium for a particular sterling option might be 1.80, and because a sterling option is for £31,250, its cost of purchase would be $562.50 (31,250 x 1.80 cents).
- Options in yen are quoted in hundredths of a cent, and so a yen option for ¥6,250,000 with a premium of 1.2 would cost $750 (6.25 million x 0.12 cents).

Philadelphia SE £/$ Options £31,250 (cents per £1)

Strike		**Calls**			**Puts**	
Price	Jul	Aug	Sep	Jul	Aug	Sep
1.550	0.57	1.33	0.83	0.72	1.48	1.95
1.560	0.24	0.92	1.40	1.38	2.06	2.46
1.570	0.06	0.61	1.04	-	2.69	3.05

Philadelphia Stock Exchange

Option	**Premium quotations**	**Minimum premium change (in cents)**	**Value per unit of change**
Sterling	Dollars/cents per £1	0.01	$3.125
Euro	Cents per €1	0.01	$6.25
Australian dollar	Cents per A$1	0.01	$5
Canadian dollar	Cents per C$1	0.01	$5
Swiss franc	Cents per SFr1	0.01	$6.25
Yen	Hundredths of a cent per yen	0.0001	$6.25
Sterling/Yen	¥ per £	¥0.02	¥625

The minimum premium change is the minimum amount by which a quoted premium can go up or down. Price changes are in multiples of this amount.

If the price of sterling put, for example, changes by the minimum amount from $0.5216 to $0.5217, the overall value or cost of the price change to the option holder/option writer is $3.125 (£31,250 x 0.01 cents per £). A price change of 0.0020 would have a value of $62.50 ($3.125 x 20).

Documentation

The buyer of a traded option receives

- written confirmation of the transaction, sent promptly by the seller, and

- periodic reports about his current options position and trading results.

Similarly, a seller of an option receives written confirmation of the transaction details. There is no option certificate that the writer or seller gives to the buyer.

Gains and Losses on Traded Options

Traded options are used in a similar way to OTC options, and can be either exercised or allowed to lapse. In addition, they can be sold before expiry at their current market value.

When the strike price (exchange rate) is specified in dollars per unit of other currency (as on the PHLX)

- an increase in the spot rate means a weakening of the dollar against the other currency
- a fall in the spot rate means a stronger dollar against the other currency.

If the spot rate is higher than the strike price on expiry, call options will be in-the-money and exercised, but put options will be out-of-the-money and allowed to lapse. If the spot rate on expiry is lower than the exercise price, put options will be in-the-money and exercised, whereas call options will be out-of-the-money and allowed to lapse.

Example
A call option on sterling against dollars has an exercise price of $1.50. On expiry the spot rate is $1.53, and the call option will be exercised because it gives the holder the right to purchase £31,250 for $46,875 (31,250 x $1.50), less than the spot price of $47,812.50 (31,250 x $1.53). In contrast, a put option on sterling at an exercise price of $1.50 would be allowed to lapse if the spot rate on expiry were $1.53, because a seller of sterling would receive more dollars by selling spot than by exercising the option.

The option holder's profit or loss on an option can be calculated in much the same way as for OTC options.

- If the option is exercised, the net profit or loss is the difference between the exercise price and the spot rate multiplied by the value of the option, minus the premium paid, minus broker's fees.
- If the option holder closes his position by selling matching options before expiry, the profit or loss is the difference between the premium paid and the premium received, minus broker's fees.
- The maximum possible loss is the premium paid, and this will occur whenever the option is not exercised.

Example

In June, an investor on the PHLX buys a euro September call option against the dollar with a strike price of $0.60 per €1. This is referred to as a euro *September 60 call.* Note that the strike price is quoted in cents per €, not in euros per dollar.

The premium is 1.6 cents per euro or $1,000 per option, value €62,500. The investor's profit or loss on the option will depend on the spot dollar/euro rate on expiry. Profit will increase by $625 (62,500 x $0.01) for each one cent increase in the margin of the spot rate over the strike price on expiry of the option.

Spot rate on expiry	**Loss**	**Profit**
Below 0.60 per €1	$1,000	
0.60 per €1	$1,000	
0.61	$375	
0.62		$250
0.63		$875
0.64		$1,500
0.65		$2,125
0.66		$2,750
0.67		$3,375

Example
In January, an investor on the PHLX buys a sterling June put option at a strike price of $1.5500. The premium is six cents, or $1,875 per option ($0.06 x 31,250).

The investor's profit or loss on the option will depend on the sterling/dollar spot rate on expiry. Profit will increase by $312.50 (31,250 x $0.01) for each one cent by which the spot price falls below the strike price.

Spot rate on expiry	Loss	Profit
Above 1.55	$1,875.0	
1.55	$1,875.0	
1.54	$1,562.5	
1.53	$1,250.0	
1.50	$312.5	
1.49		0
1.48		$312.5
1.45		$1,250.0

Writing Options
The traded options market gives investors the opportunity to make a return from writing options. To sell an option without having previously purchased a matching option, in effect, is to write an option.

For the investment in a margin deposit with the options exchange, an investor can hope to make a relatively large return in a fairly short time. Provided the option is not exercised, the investment return

- will be the premium received for writing the option, and
- will be earned when the option expires.

The investment risk, however, is that the option will be exercised, and the option writer will make a loss.

Example
When the euro/dollar exchange is €1 = $1.03, an investor has €250,000. The dollar equivalent of €250,000 is $257,500 that can be invested at 5% per annum.

The investor writes four, three-month at-the-money euro call options, and receives total premiums of $5,150.

The investor converts his €250,000 into dollars and invests them at 5% per annum.

Analysis
If the options were not exercised, the investor's return from writing the options will be

$$\frac{\$5{,}150}{\$257{,}500} \times \frac{12}{3} \times 100\% = 8\% \text{ per annum}$$

	% per annum
Yield from investing dollars	5
Yield from writing options	8
Total yield	13

If the exchange rate moves in the option holder's favor, and the option is exercised at expiry, the investor can use the $150,000 on deposit in settlement of the option. The three-month yield would then be just 5%.

Writing Naked Options
A high-risk investment strategy, using the previous example, would be to write four three-month euro call options, and earn a premium of $5,150, but without having $257,500 on deposit to cover the possibility that the option will be exercised. The investor would then be hoping to earn a return of $5,150 for an investment of just the margin deposited with the options exchange. The risk is that the option will be exercised, and the option writer will have to buy the dollars to settle his obligations, leaving a loss on the options investment. This high-risk investment strategy is known as writing uncovered options or writing naked options.

Traded Options and OTC Options Compared

Banks use exchange-traded options to hedge their OTC currency exposures and there is a close link between the OTC and the exchange-traded markets. A comparison of standardized traded options and OTC options is given in the summary table. However, since PHLX introduced customized FX options, the contrast between OTC and traded options has become much more blurred. OTC options have several advantages, especially for large non-bank corporates that use options to hedge currency exposures.

- OTC options give flexibility of amount, maturity date and strike price, although flexibility can be achieved with traded options by closing a position before the expiry date.
- OTC options allow large amounts of currency in a single trade.
- OTC options allow more scope to transact long-dated, 18-month plus, options, although long-dated options are now traded on the PHLX.

OTC vs. Exchange-traded Standardized Options Characteristics

OTC	Exchange-traded
Negotiated with a bank	Bought through a broker on an exchange market
Any amount of currency, to suit the option buyer's specific requirements	Standard amount or multiples of a standard amount
Any convertible currency	Only major currencies traded, largely involving the dollar, e.g. yen, sterling, etc
Specific expiry date to suit the option buyer. This can be longer term than exchange-traded options	Standard expiry dates: third Wednesday of March, June, September, December

Any strike price can be agreed, although the premium will be fixed according to the strike price	Strike prices at fixed intervals
Premium usually is paid one or two days after transaction. Delivery of currency usually is one or two days after exercise	Premium paid on day of transactions Tradeable during tenor. Options can be sold as well as purchased at any time when the exchange is open
Arranged for specific customer. Not negotiable. Cannot be on-sold. Redeemable if unwanted before expiry date, but only at the bank that wrote the option	Used by non-banks and also for interbank deals. OTC options encourage a stronger bank/ customer relationship. Used mainly by banks to hedge positions taken with their OTC deals. Used by only the largest companies in Europe, usually in large sums of between $5-10 million

The main disadvantage of OTC options to the non-bank corporate is the difficulty of putting a value to its option positions, particularly if the option is not of the plain vanilla type. For traded options, positions are more easily valued from the current market prices.

9

Second and Third Generation Options Packages

There are a number of sophisticated options products that are available either as packaged products from banks or self-assembled by large companies with a quasi bank-dealing capability. These are referred to collectively as second or third generation packages.

Second Generation Options Packages

Second generation products normally consist of a combination of a written and a purchased option.

- An option is written and the premium is received.
- This premium income is applied to the purchase of an option at a different strike rate.

The net effect is a low-cost or even a zero-cost options package for the customer, and second generation options were devised to overcome the reluctance of customers to pay up front the premium for option cover.

For second generation products the written and the purchased options normally have the same maturity/expiry date.

However, the term option can be misleading for some of these packages because some such write/buy combinations are a surrogate forward exchange contract, under which currency conversion is obligatory, not optional, with only the precise rate being determined on maturity, depending on the prevailing spot market exchange rate.

With other second generation packages, the option really is an option, but the strike price is heavily adjusted to compensate the bank for a reduced front-end premium payment. Second generation products include

- Boston option
- compound option
- participating forward contract.

Boston Option

A Boston option, also known as a break forward contract or a forward reversing option, is a mixture of a currency option and a forward contract. A contract is made to buy (or sell) a quantity of currency at an agreed future date. The rate of exchange is

- the forward rate plus
- an option premium.

The option is to sell back or buy back the currency at the forward rate. No premium is payable. If this option is not exercised on expiry, the sale or purchase of the currency will go ahead at the contracted rate (forward rate + option premium).

Example
A large UK company arranges a Boston option with a bank to sell $20 million six months' forward. The rate in the contract is $1.50, consisting of the six-month forward rate of $1.48 plus an option premium of $0.02.

Outcome 1
At maturity, if the spot rate is less than $1.48, the dollar having strengthened in value, the company will want to sell the dollars spot rather than at the forward rate.

- The company will sell $20 million at $1.50, under the forward contract agreement.

- It will also exercise its option to buy back $20 million at $1.48.
- It will sell the $20 million it needs at the spot rate that is more favorable than $1.48.

For example, if the spot rate is $1.45, the company will

	£
Sell $20 million at the contracted rate of $1.50	+13,333,333
Exercise its option to buy back the $20 million at the forward rate of $1.48	-13,513,514
Sell the $20 million at the spot rate of $1.45	+13,793,103
Net proceeds	+13,612,922

The net proceeds provide an effective exchange rate of about $1.47 ($20 million ÷ £13,612,922).

Outcome 2

At maturity, if the spot rate is more than $1.48, the company will not exercise its option, and will sell $20 million at $1.50 as contracted.

The effect of a Boston option is, in effect, to obtain a currency option but also to defer the payment of the premium until maturity. In this example the company must sell the dollars at $1.50 whatever the outcome, thereby securing income of $0.02 (the cost of the premium) for the bank on expiry.

Compound Option

Compound options, or options on options, are options to buy or sell options, i.e. options on options. They can be used to hedge against the risk of adverse movements in option premiums.

Example

The current premium on a three-month dollar call option might be 1.5%. A company treasurer wants to purchase a three-month dollar call option, but not until next month, and he is worried about a big increase in the option premium before then.

He might be able to arrange a compound option whereby the bank, for a further premium of 0.5%, will grant the company an option to purchase a call option for a premium of 1.5%.

Cost of compound premium	0.5%
Cost of currency option premium	1.5%
	2.0%

The maximum total cost of premium that the treasurer has secured will be 2%.

The company will not exercise the compound option in one month's time if the premium on a three-month dollar call has fallen to less than 1.5%. It will exercise the compound option if the premium is over 1.5%, and will have made an overall profit on its hedge if the premium is over 2%. For example, if the premium is

- 2.4%, the company will exercise the option and pay 1.5%
- 1.8%, the company will exercise the option and pay 1.5%
- 1.2%, the company will let the option lapse and pay 1.2%.

Participating Forward Contract

A participating forward contract is a form of currency option, in spite of its name, although no up-front premium is payable. Instead, the bank obtains the right to share some of the benefits to the company of any exchange rate movements in its favor. The premium is in effect built into the rate at which the bank will share any profits.

Example
A UK company needs to purchase $30 million in six months' time. Its treasurer would like to hedge the currency risk, and prefers the idea of an out-of-the-money option, securing a worst-case exchange rate that is no worse than the strike price. However, he doesn't want to pay a premium for his option. A six-month forward exchange contract rate would be $1.4950.

The company might arrange a participating forward contract whereby

- it obtains a six-month call option on the $30 million at $1.47, that being the worst possible exchange rate that the company wants, and
- it sells to the bank a six-month put option for a proportion of the $30 million, perhaps 25% or $7.5 million at a strike price of $1.52.

Analysis

If the spot rate in six months is less than the call option rate of $1.47, the dollar having strengthened, the company will exercise its option to buy the $30 million at $1.47.

If the spot rate is above $1.47 and below $1.52, the company will choose to buy at the spot rate and not at $1.47. It will not exercise its option.

If the spot rate is above $1.52 the bank will exercise its option to sell $7.5 million at $1.52. In effect, the company can buy $22.5m of the $30m that it requires at the spot rate but must buy $7.5m at the less favorable rate of $1.52.

Third Generation Options Products

Third generation products are more sophisticated still. Like second generation products, they consist of buy/write packages but the maturity timing of the call and the put options is mismatched. A package might consist of the purchase of a long-dated option and the writing of a rolling series of shorter-dated options to cover the cost. While second generation options are branded products with proprietary names, third generation products are of such limited appeal that they tend to be customized for each large company or bank that is interested in them.

Financial managers should be aware of the precise consequences of transacting second or third generation options products because the cost of the package is usually more expensive than the sum of the parts. This is to compensate the bank for the time and money spent devising the product and the administrative hassle of transacting and managing the package. Unless there is a clear purpose and advantage to be obtained, these products should be avoided.

Exotic Options

Some banks write a variety of other options with special features. They are sometimes referred to as exotic options, to describe their unusual characteristics. These include

- Asian options (or average options)
- lookback options, and
- barrier options.

Asian options apply an averaging process to either the spot price or to the exercise price, to determine whether the option is in-the-money and what the settlement should be if the option is exercised.

- For one type of Asian option, the exercise price is compared, not with the spot rate on expiry, but with the average (daily) spot rate over the life of the option.
- For a second type of Asian option, the exercise price is calculated as the average spot rate over the life of the option. If this is more favorable to the option holder than the spot rate at expiry, the option will be exercised.

Lookback options apply either an exercise price or a spot rate that makes it more likely that the option will be exercised.

- For one type of lookback option, the exercise price on expiry is compared with the most favorable spot rate, i.e. the spot rate offering the largest payout to the option holder, that existed at any time during the life of the option.
- For a second type of lookback option, the exercise price is the most favorable spot rate to the option holder that existed at any

time during the life of the option.

Barrier options are regular options with the added feature that they lapse or come into being only if the spot price passes through a specified level (barrier).

A down-and-out option will expire if the spot rate falls below a specified barrier level. An up-and-out option will expire if the spot rate moves above a barrier. A down-and-in option comes into being if the spot rate falls below a barrier, and an up-and-in option comes into being if the spot moves above a barrier.

Guidelines for Buying Options

A large company is in a much better position than a small company to buy options. It has ready access to knowledgeable staff in banks in a big financial center and to traded options brokers. However, small companies normally will have to rely on the service from the staff of their local bank who might not be familiar with options, and so their access to OTC or traded options might be constrained.

Consequently the following suggestions on how to set about buying an option differ between large and small companies.

OTC Options and the Large Company

It is important to be properly prepared before picking up the phone to buy an option from a bank or broker. Without preparation, mistakes are more likely to happen.

Preparing to Deal

The company dealer should first calculate the cost of each point of price in terms of total money value in order to measure the effect of price differentials on quotes. The process of trying to squeeze an extra basis point or two out of a bank is a waste of time and effort if it is worth only a small amount of money, but clearly worthwhile if hundreds or thousands of dollars are at stake. For example, for an option to purchase $5 million from a UK bank, each one basis point (0.01%) on the premium will cost £333 at a strike rate of $1.50 = £1. Similarly, for a premium that is quoted in pence per dollar, each tenth of a penny per dollar on the price would cost £5,000 for an option on $5 million.

The dealer should select a group of banks to invite to tender. The banks that are most price competitive on OTC options are largely the group of banks that are major players in the forward foreign exchange markets. The investment banks are less inclined to apply their capital to run a book in long-dated forward contracts but are prepared to make markets in the more profitable options market.

It is inadvisable to invite more than *three* banks to quote on a large transaction. This is because by phoning round a number of banks, a customer will allow time for the first banks that are approached to sound out other market-makers in options for prices at which they could lay off or pass on part or all of the transaction at a profit. When several banks do this at the same time for the one deal, other banks in the market will assume that there are several transactions about to hit the market, and adjust their prices by a significant amount in anticipation of an approach from one or more of the assumed customers.

Dealing

Even if the company is seeking an at-the-money spot (ATMS) strike price, its dealer should begin by specifying a particular strike price rather than inviting banks to quote at the prevailing spot price because the spot price will fluctuate by the minute and make direct price comparisons between different banks impossible. Option pricing by banks involves running a computer model and this process can take at least ten minutes before the bank responds with a price. By specifying a fixed strike price, the company can compare quoted premiums during the ten to 15 minutes it takes for the banks to assemble their quotes.

Then the company dealer can select the most competitive price and ask that bank to requote at a strike price equal to the now prevailing spot rate, so that it can buy an option at-the-money.

The dealer should indicate that he expects the quote from a bank to be good for a period of 15 minutes or so, provided market conditions are stable, to give himself time to get quotes from other banks.

If a company wants to use an option to lock in a worst possible exchange rate for a future foreign currency transaction, for example to fix a minimum amount of local currency income from an anticipated amount of foreign currency revenue, it can select the strike price that will give it this worst possible rate.

For instance, if a UK company expects to receive $510,600 in three months' time, that it will sell in exchange for sterling, it might want to ensure that it receives at least £340,000. If it anticipates a premium of about £5,000, it will need income of £345,000 from selling the dollars to obtain net income of £340,000.

The company could ask for a strike price of $1.48 or less (510,600 ÷ 345,000) for a put option on the dollars, provided that the actual premium quoted is £5,000 or lower.

It is important to confirm that an OTC option would be preferable in each instance to hedging with a forward contract.

The dealer should ask for two-way quotes, call and put options and monitor the spread quoted by that particular bank. Keeping a record of all quotes will allow the company to carry out periodic reviews of pricing efficiency on every bank on its list of potential counterparties for options.

A dealer might ask for quotes as a *percentage of the nominal value of the option to be transacted* to avoid confusion about the pricing basis. However, banks might quote in money amounts, i.e. so many cents per pound or so many euros per pound, rather than in percentages.

An American OTC option gives its holder greater flexibility than a European OTC option in the choice of exercise date, but the premium will be higher.

The OTC market for European options normally is sufficiently liquid for an option holder to redeem an unwanted option at a reasonable price, for example, the bank might pay more than the original premium when the option is in-the-money, and companies will often save money by purchasing European rather than American options.

OTC Options and the Small Company

It is unusual for a small company to have more than one relationship bank. The small company is likely to be obliged to buy an OTC option without any choice of bank as option writer. The company should try to obtain the best terms, i.e. the lowest premium, from its bank, but, unlike large companies that have several relationship banks, it cannot apply the threat of taking its options business to a competitor.

Preparing to Deal

The finance director or financial controller should first establish that the company's bank is prepared to write OTC options. To win the bank's consent, it will be necessary to explain why the company wishes to buy OTC options, which currencies are involved, and the likely dealing dates/expiry dates. A meeting probably will be needed with the branch manager and the branch official with responsibility for foreign exchange.

This meeting also would provide an opportunity to establish clearly the procedures that would apply for transacting OTC options with the bank. For example

- nominating the official(s) in the company with authority to deal with the bank in options, and the official(s) at the bank with which the company would deal
- specifying how an option would be purchased or exercised
- specifying what documentary confirmation would be required for purchase or exercise.

The premium for an option will be decided by the bank's central dealing room that will also write the option. The branch will act as a go-between for the company. The company is more likely to avoid excessive premiums if the branch will agree to quote the premium before the option is written by the central dealing room, instead of expecting instructions from the company to deal on a best-efforts basis at a price that will not be reported before the transaction is made.

When the company wishes to buy an OTC option under its arrangement with the bank, its dealer, the financial director or financial controller, should explain to the nominated branch official the reasons for the proposed transaction. This official should then be able to confirm that the transaction would achieve its desired end, thus giving reassurance that the company has not made a mistake. If the company doubts the advice, opinion or ability of the branch official, it should refuse to deal and instead write to the bank

- giving the details and intention of the desired transaction, and
- requesting to deal directly with expert banking staff at regional office or the bank's central dealing room.

Example
A small US company might write to its bank giving advance notification of its intention to buy an OTC option in respect of an order by the company to purchase machine tools from a Japanese supplier, payable in yen. There should be no dispute about blame if a transaction is arranged in which the company buys a put option on yen against dollars instead of a call option. The blame would lie with the bank.

Dealing
The bank's preference is likely to be for the company to allow it to arrange an option on an at-best or best-efforts basis, i.e. at a suitable price for market conditions prevailing at the time the option is transacted. This arrangement would not allow the company the opportunity to decline the transaction if the option premium is too high. At the very least, the company should ask for an indication of the option premium when communicating the details of the proposed transaction to its local branch.

If the transaction is of significant size relative to the size of the company's business, it is not unreasonable to seek direct access to the bank's central dealing room in order to decide at the time of dealing whether the premium is acceptable.

If the price is unacceptable, the company can indicate its required level of premium and ask the bank to monitor market prices and transact the option if and when the target price is achievable.

Once an option has been transacted it is important that the company checks carefully on receipt the written confirmation of the terms of the transaction. Mistakes are best rectified as soon as possible.

Exchange-traded Options

For both large and small companies wishing to buy exchange-traded options, a decision has to be made about which options exchange, or exchanges, should be used for dealing in options in particular currencies. Most exchange-traded currency options are options on currency futures that are traded on the IMM division of the Chicago Mercantile Exchange. Options on currency futures are not described in this book.

Options on major currencies against the dollar generally are available at all leading options exchanges but cross-currency options tend to be more of a local offering.

The company must then obtain access to the selected exchange via a recognized broker, possibly a major bank or a specialist broking firm.

11

Option-dealing Strategies

Banks (and other options traders) expose themselves to the risk of losses when they write options. Losses can be large unless measures are taken to contain them. Consequently, banks pursue various option-dealing strategies to control the risks, involving combinations of option writing and option buying. Similarly, investors in traded options can adopt strategies to control their investment risk. A few strategies are discussed briefly here to illustrate how banks can try to limit their risks.

Option-dealing strategies are commonly pursued by buying and selling exchange-traded options. Because the Philadelphia Stock Exchange is the world's leading market for traded currency options, those options will be used in the examples that follow. It is also important to note that for options involving dollars, exchange rates are quoted in dollar terms; for example, exercise prices for euro options (and spot rates) are quoted in cents per euro.

- An increase in the spot price will increase the market price of a call option (in sterling or yen, etc.).
- A fall in the spot rate will increase the value of a put option.

Vertical Bull Spread

This strategy, also known as a bullish call spread, is based on the view that the spot rate is likely to rise. A dealer will

- write a call option at one strike price, and
- buy a call option for the same amount of currency and the same expiry date, at a lower strike price.

The sale of the option at the higher strike price helps to offset the cost of the premium for buying the call option at the lower strike price. This restricts the maximum potential loss. The potential profit from the strategy, however, is also limited by the option that is written at the higher strike price.

A vertical bull spread strategy therefore has a maximum potential profit, but also a maximum potential loss. The maximum profit is earned if the spot price were above the higher exercise price at expiry.

Example
A dealer writes June call options for Swiss francs against dollars at a strike price of $0.60. The premium is $750 per option contract. The dealer then buys the same number of June call options at a lower strike price of, for example, $0.57 and the premium paid is $1,625 per contract.

Analysis
If the spot rate moved above $0.60, both options would be exercised. The dealer will make a profit from the difference between the strike prices of the purchased and the written options (in this example $0.03 per SFr1 on each option for SFr62,500), minus the net premium paid.

For example, if the spot price at expiry were $0.62 = SFr1, both call options would be exercised.

		Per option
	$	$
Profit on purchased call option		
($0.62 - $0.57) x 62,500		3,125
Loss on written call option		
($0.62 - $0.60) x 62,500		-1,250
		1,875
Premium paid for purchased option	1,625	
Premium received for written option	750	
Net premium paid		-875
Overall profit		1,000

This is the maximum profit that the dealer can make, because if the spot price is higher on expiry, the profit on the purchased option minus the loss on the written option will still be just $1,875.

If the spot rate on expiry were below the lower strike price of the two options, neither option would be exercised. The dealer's loss would be the net premium paid, in this example $875. This is the maximum loss that could occur.

If the spot rate on expiry were between the strike prices of the two options, the dealer would exercise the purchased call option, and make a profit, but the written option would not be exercised. There would be an overall profit or loss after deducting the net premium paid.

For example, if the spot rate on expiry were $0.59 = SFr1, the dealer would make a profit of $0.02 per franc on the purchased call option, or $1,250 per option contract. After deducting the net premium of $875, there would be an overall profit of $375 per option.

The loss or profit from the vertical bull spread strategy in this example is illustrated in the following diagram.

Profit or Loss from Vertical Bull Spread Strategy

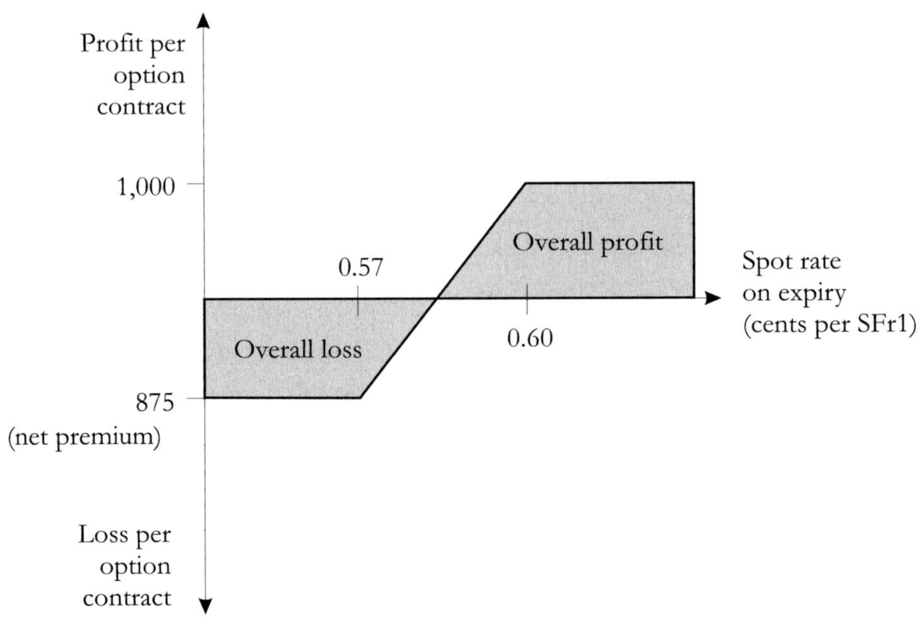

Vertical Bear Spread

This strategy, also called a bearish put spread, is based on the view that the exchange rate will fall. A dealer will

- write a put option at one strike price, and
- purchase a put option at a higher strike price, for the same amount of currency and the same expiry date.

The strategy is similar in concept to a vertical bull spread, except that it is based on put options and an expectation of a fall in the exchange rate.

The maximum loss from the strategy is the difference between the premium paid for buying the option and the (lower) premium received for writing the option at the lower strike price. The potential profit is limited by the option written at the higher strike price.

Example

A dealer, anticipating a fall in the value of sterling against the dollar, writes a March put option at a strike price of $1.500, for a premium of 4.80 cents per £1. The premium for an option on £31,250 therefore would be $1,500. The dealer also purchases a March put option at a higher strike price of $1.550, for a premium of 8.0 cents per £1 ($2,500 per contract).

Analysis

If the spot price on expiry is below $1.500, both options will be exercised. The dealer will make a profit from the difference between the two strike prices, in this example $0.05 per £1 on each option contract of £31,250, minus the net premium paid.

For example, if the spot rate on expiry is $1.480, both put options will be exercised.

Profit or Loss from Vertical Bull Spread Strategy

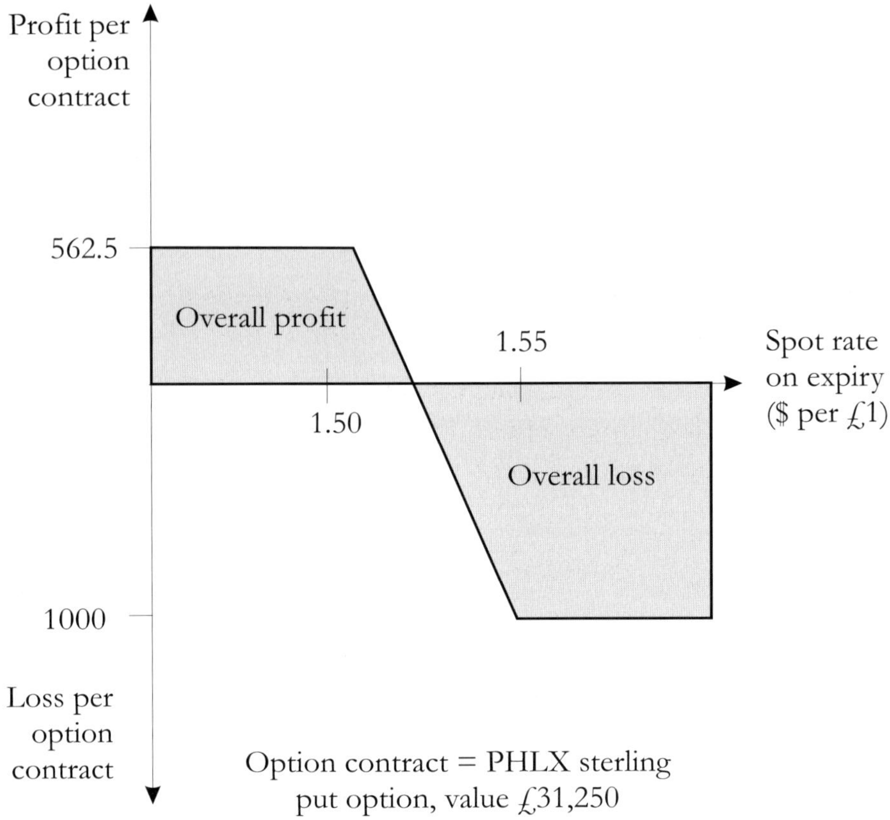

		Per option
	$	$
Profit on purchased put option		
($1.550 - $1.480) x 31,250		2,187.5
Loss on written put option		
($1.500 - $1.480) x 31,250		-625.0
		1,562.5
Premium paid for purchased option	2,500	
Premium received for written option	1,500	
Net premium paid		-1,000.0
Overall profit		562.5

The $562.50 is the maximum profit under this dealing strategy.

If the spot rate on expiry were above the higher of the two strike prices, in this example $1.550, neither put option would be exercised and the dealer would make a loss of the net premium paid, that at $1,000 is the maximum loss under this option-dealing strategy.

If the spot rate on expiry were between the two strike prices, the dealer would exercise the purchased put option, but would allow the written option to lapse. The dealer's profit on the purchased option minus the net premium paid ($1,000) gives an overall profit or loss per contract.

The loss or profit from the vertical bull spread strategy in this example is illustrated in the diagram on the previous page.

Volatility Trades

Vertical bull spread and vertical bear spread strategies are based on a view of the likely movement, up or down, in the exchange rate. A different type of option-dealing strategy is to take a view on the *volatility* of exchange rate movements, both up *and* down. A dealer can base a strategy on either of two opposite views, that

- exchange rate movements up to expiry date will be large (volatility will be high), or
- exchange rate movements up to expiry date will be small (volatility will be low).

Straddle

A straddle is the name given to a position where the options trader expects an increase in the exchange rate volatility and so buys a put and a call at the same strike price and with the same expiry date, i.e. he buys a straddle. The strike price will be at-the-money close to it. If the exchange rate moves sufficiently, either up or down, the trader will end up in profit.

Example
A trader on the PHLX buys a March £1.50 put for 2.70 cents and a March £1.50 call for 3.20 cents.

Remember that with sterling options on the PHLX, a call option is an option to buy sterling and a put option is an option to sell sterling in exchange for dollars.

The combined cost of the premiums is 5.90 cents. This is the maximum loss that occurs if the exchange rate were $1.50 on expiry, and neither option were exercised. If the exchange rate were above or below $1.50, the trader would exercise either the call or the put option.

- For example, if the spot exchange rate were $1.57 on expiry, the trader would exercise the call option to buy sterling for dollars at $1.50 to £1, and would immediately sell the sterling at $1.57 to make a profit of seven cents per £1. The net profit after deducting the option premiums of 5.9 cents would be 1.1 cents per £1.
- If the spot rate were $1.45 on expiry, the trader would exercise the put option to sell sterling for dollars at $1.50, and simultaneously buy back the sterling at the spot price to make a profit of five cents per £1. There would be a net loss in this example, however, after option premiums are deducted, of 0.9 cents per £1.

To make an overall profit on this straddle strategy after deducting premium costs, the spot exchange rate would have to move to below $1.4410 ($1.50 - 0.059) when the call option would be exercised, or above $1.5590 ($1.50 + 0.059) when the put option would be exercised.

To make a profit, volatility in the exchange rate would have to be high, because at an exchange rate between 1.4410 - 1.5590 on expiry, the trader would make a net loss.

Straddle Strategy

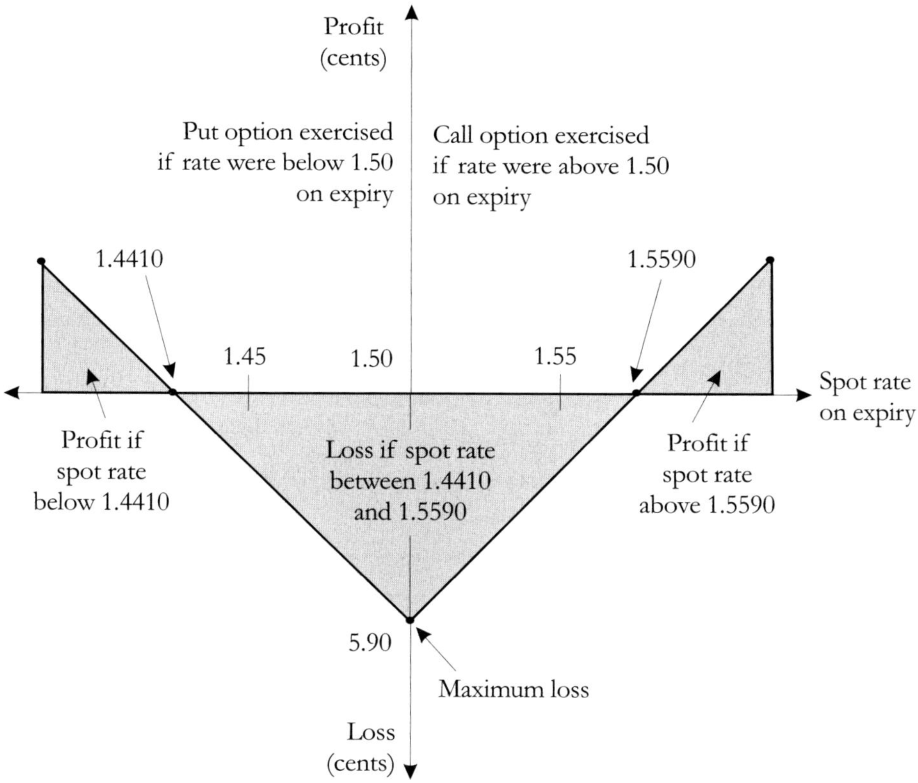

Straddle Write (or Short Straddle)

This strategy is similar in concept to a straddle, except that the trader expects a fall in the exchange rate volatility and the exchange rate to be fairly stable. The trader therefore *writes* a put and a call at the same strike price and for the same expiry date, i.e. he writes a straddle. The strike price will be at-the-money or close to it.

Example

A trader on the PHLX writes a March £1.50 put for 2.70 cents and a March £1.50 call for 3.20 cents. The combined earnings from the premiums is 5.90 cents, and this is the maximum profit that the trader can make. This profit would be earned if the exchange rate on expiry were exactly \$1.50.

If the spot rate on expiry were above \$1.50, the put option would be exercised by the option holder and the trader would make some loss (ignoring the premium earned); similarly, if the exchange rate on expiry were below \$1.50, the call option would be exercised by the option holder and the trader would make some loss (ignoring the premium earned).

To make an overall profit on the straddle write strategy, the exchange rate on expiry should not differ from the strike price by more than 5.90 cents (the earnings from the premiums combined).

For example, if the spot rate on expiry were \$1.47 (below the strike price by \$0.03) the holder of the put option would exercise the right to sell sterling at \$1.50 because this will earn more dollars than selling sterling at the spot rate. The option holder would make a profit and the trader (as option writer) would make a loss of three cents per £1. The holder of the call option would not exercise his option, however, and so the trader's net profit of 2.9 cents per £1 comes from the premiums earned of 5.9 cents minus the loss on the put option.

The profit/loss earned will vary with the spot rate on expiry as illustrated in the graph on the following page. Notice that it is a mirror image of the long straddle strategy because the trader is speculating on low volatility here, rather than on high volatility in the case of the long straddle position.

Straddle Write Strategy

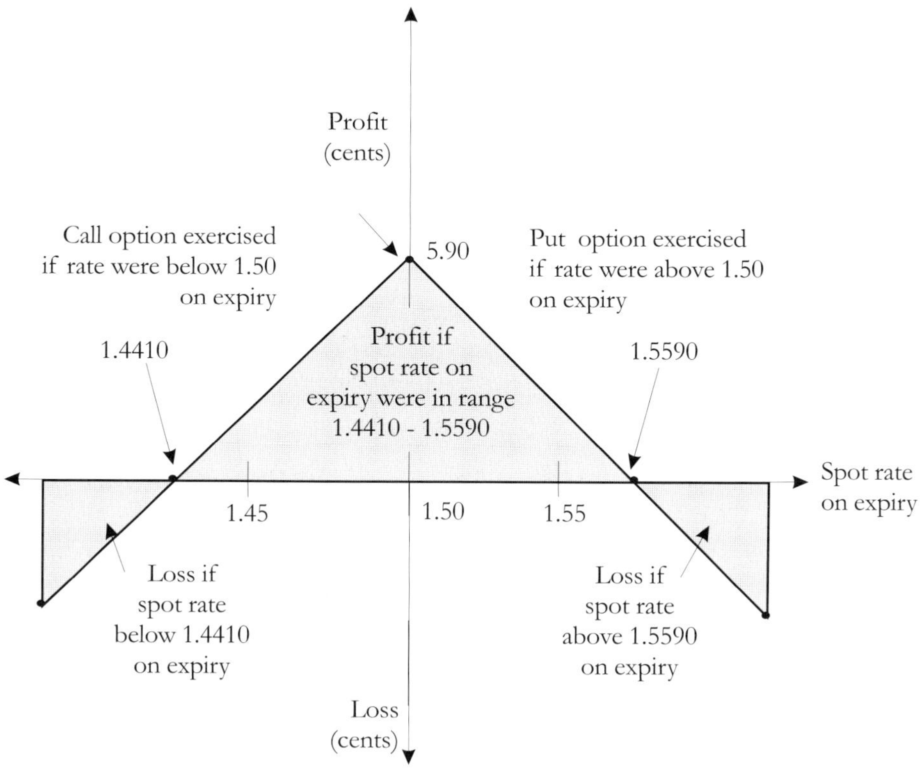

Arbitrage

Arbitrage is a term referring to a trading strategy in which the trader seeks to make a profit from buying or selling the same or similar items, in different markets, at prices that give him/her the opportunity for an immediate and certain profit. In the context of foreign currency, traders might see an opportunity for profit from dealing in the spot or forward currency markets, in currency options or in the currency futures markets. Profit would be made purely on the price difference between buying and selling.

Arbitrage opportunities are quickly exploited, and because market prices also react quickly to buying and selling orders, favorable price differences and hence arbitrage opportunities do not last long.

Arbitrage opportunities sometimes can be exploited by treasurers of large non-bank corporates, not just by dealers in banks, but the advent of computer monitoring on cross-market pricing means that risk-free arbitrage transactions are the preserve of only the most sophisticated players in the market.

Appendix: Mathematics of Option Pricing

This appendix describes the mathematics of option pricing models.

Although it is useful to study the mathematical concepts in options pricing, mathematics can be difficult to comprehend. Therefore this appendix uses simplified explanations and simplifying assumptions, where possible, to make the text more comprehensible.

The purpose of this appendix is three-fold

- to illustrate how volatility is measured, and what this measurement signifies
- to describe a simple option pricing model for an at-the-money option that also illustrates a delta hedging position
- to describe a more complex currency option pricing model, based on the Black-Scholes model.

Measuring Volatility

The volatility of an exchange rate can be measured mathematically from historical price data.

A simplified example, based on a very short time period, will be used to illustrate the mathematics.

Example
The sterling/dollar spot rate at the close of London trading on each of seven successive trading days was

Day	Closing rate
1	1.4820
2	1.4750
3	1.4705
4	1.4815
5	1.4825
6	1.4800
7	1.4710

Analysis

The first step in measuring volatility is to obtain measurements for the daily change in the exchange rate. We are not trying to monitor the exchange rate. It is the amount and direction of change that are significant.

Change in price can be measured as a price relative. This is the ratio of the price on one day to the price on the previous day.

Each price relative is then converted into its natural logarithm value, you might have a calculator that computes natural logarithms. The price relatives and their natural logarithm values are shown in the table

Day	Price	Price relative	Natural logarithm of price relative
(d)		(d+1) ÷ (d)	(x)
1	1.4820	-	-
2	1.4750	0.9953	-0.0047
3	1.4705	0.9969	-0.0031
4	1.4815	1.0075	0.0075
5	1.4825	1.0007	0.0007
6	1.4800	0.9983	-0.0017
7	1.4710	0.9939	-0.0061

The average (mean) value of the natural logarithms of the price relatives, $\bar{x}$, is calculated.

$$\frac{-0.0047 - 0.0031 + 0.0075 + 0.0007 - 0.0017 - 0.0061}{6} = -0.00123$$

We can calculate a standard deviation of the natural logarithms of the price relatives as

$$\sigma = \sqrt{\frac{1}{(n - 1)} (x - \overline{x})^2}$$

where n is the number of natural logarithm values used in calculating volatility.

x	$x - \overline{x}$	$x - \overline{x}^2$
-0.0047	-0.00347	0.00001204
-0.0031	-0.00187	0.00000350
0.0075	0.00873	0.00007621
0.0007	0.00193	0.00000372
-0.0017	-0.00047	0.00000022
-0.0061	-0.00487	0.00002372
		0.00011941

$$\sigma = \sqrt{\frac{0.00011941}{(6 - 1)}} = \sqrt{0.000023882} = 0.0049 \text{ approximately}$$

The volatility over a longer period can be estimated as:

$$\sigma \sqrt{d}$$

where d is the number of days in the period.

For example, if a year has 250 FX trading days and daily volatility in the exchange rate is 0.0049, annual volatility is 0.0075 ($0.0049 \times \sqrt{250}$), i.e. 7.75%.

The Meaning of Volatility

Volatility is measured as a standard deviation of price relatives, and it is assumed that price changes are normally distributed. This means that if annual volatility in an exchange rate were estimated as 7.75% and today's closing exchange rate were 1.4710, there is

- a 67% probability that the exchange rate in one year's time will be within the range ±1 standard deviation of today's rate, i.e. within the range of ±7.75% from 1.4710 that is 1.3570 to 1.5850

- a 95% probability that the exchange rate in one year's time will be within ±1.96 standard deviations of today's rate

There are different ways of measuring volatility. For example, the period of time over which price changes are monitored can vary. Each bank writing currency options could have its own measurement of volatility for any exchange rate. The basic principles of measurement are covered by the example above.

Changes in Volatility over Time

Volatility is measured from historical data as a means of predicting future price changes. However, over time the price volatility of an exchange rate will change, sometimes by a large amount. So it is important to measure volatility continually, incorporating the most recent price change information.

Further Aspects of Volatility Measurement

Volatility measures the rate of change in market price, e.g. exchange rate, and also the uncertainty about the direction and size of change.

- If an exchange rate were fixed, without any fluctuation at all, volatility would be zero.
- If an exchange rate were to rise by the same percentage amount every day, e.g. by 0.1% every day, volatility also would be zero.
- If an exchange rate were to rise by 2% one day and rose by 1% the next day, volatility over this two-day period would be less than if the exchange rate were to rise by 2% one day and then fall by 1% the next day. This is because volatility is higher when the direction as well as the amount of price change is more variable.

Example

The sterling/dollar exchange rate on Day 1 is £1 = $1.5000. It rises by 3% the next day (Day 2) to $1.5450.

Analysis

If the exchange rate were to rise by a further 1% on Day 3 to $1.5604, two-day volatility would be 1.39%, measured as follows

Day	**Rate**	**Price relative**	**Natural logarithm**		
			x	$x - \bar{x}$	$x - \bar{x}^2$
1	1.5000				
2	1.5450	1.03	0.02956	0.0098	0.000096
3	1.5604	1.01	0.00995	0.0098	0.000096
			0.03951		0.000192
			0.01976		

$$\text{2-day volatility} = \sqrt{\frac{0.000192}{1}} = 0.0139 \text{ or } 1.39\%$$

If the exchange rate were to have *fallen* by 1% on Day 3, from $1.5450 to $1.5295 the two-day volatility would have been higher, 2.8%, measured as follows

Day	**Rate**	**Price relative**	**Natural logarithm**		
			x	$x - \bar{x}$	$x - \bar{x}^2$
1	1.5000				
2	1.5450	1.03	0.02956	0.0198	0.00039
3	1.5295	0.99	-0.01005	-0.0198	0.00039
			0.01951		0.00078

$$\bar{x} = 0.00976$$

$$\text{Volatility } \sigma = \sqrt{\frac{0.00078}{1}} = 0.028 \text{ or } 2.8\%$$

The higher volatility reflects the difference in the price change, 2% on Day 3 compared with 3% on Day 2, and also the reverse direction of the price change, i.e. the fall on Day 3.

If the exchange rate were to have risen by 3% on Day 3, from $1.5450 to $1.5913, i.e. by the same percentage change as on Day 2, two-day volatility would have been zero.

Day	Rate	Price rclative	Natural logarithm x	$x - \bar{x}$	$x - \bar{x}^2$
1	1.5000				
2	1.5450	1.03	0.02956	0	0
3	1.5913	1.03	0.02956	0	0
			0.05912		0

$$\bar{x} = 0.02956$$

$$\text{Volatility} \quad \sigma = \sqrt{0} = 0$$

In contrast, a *fall* in the exchange rate on Day 3, back to $1.5000, would have given a two-day volatility of about 6%.

Using Volatility

The volatility of an exchange rate affects the time value of a currency option, and can be an important factor in the pricing of an option. Pricing formulae for currency options include volatility as a variable in the pricing equation.

Two options pricing models are explained in the remainder of this appendix.

A Simple Options Pricing Model

A simple options pricing model can be used to obtain

- the minimum premium to be charged by the option writer, and
- the delta hedge required.

The model will be explained with a numerical example. Some simplifying assumptions have been made, but the model remains a reasonably accurate guide to pricing at-the-money options, or options that are nearly at-the-money.

The example prices a call option, but the same principles can be applied to put options.

Example

A bank has been asked to write a European dollar call option against Swiss francs, for expiry in three months. The option is on $100,000 and the exercise price will be at-the-money (forward). The premium is payable in Swiss francs. Current exchange rates and interest rates are

Spot rate	$1 = SFr1.7366
Three-month forward rate	$1 = SFr1.7480
Three-month $ interest rate	3 1/8%
Three-month SFr interest rate	5 3/4%

Volatility for the dollar/Swiss franc exchange rate is 4% over three months and 8% over 12 months.

The bank will hedge its risk by buying dollars, selling Swiss francs, three months forward.

Analysis

The bank can establish a price for the option on the basis that

- it will hedge its risk by buying dollars, selling Swiss francs, forward, and
- if the spot rate in three months were either 4% above or below the current spot rate, it would make neither a profit nor a loss on the option, taking into consideration the profit or loss on the hedging action: 4% equals one times volatility in the three-month period to expiry of the option.

The purpose of the hedge is to create an offsetting profit if the bank were to make a loss on writing the option, i.e. if the option were exercised. The dollars purchased three months forward could be used either in settlement of the option or could be resold at the new spot price at a profit.

However, if the option were not exercised, there would be a loss on the dollars purchased (Swiss francs sold) forward. The dollars could be resold at the spot price, but only for less than they cost to buy.

The calculations below show how the bank will breakeven if the spot rate at expiry of the option were 4% higher or 4% lower than the outright forward price when the option was written. The market's expectation should be that the spot rate at expiry of the option would be more or less the same as the forward rate when the option was written.

Forward spot rate (= option exercise price)	1.7480
If 4% higher, rate	1.7480 x 1.04 = 1.8179
If 4% lower, rate	1.7480/1.04 = 1.6808

Note: 4% = volatility over the period to expiry.

Exercise price 1.7480	**At expiry, spot rate = 1.8179**	**At expiry, spot rate = 1.6808**
Option exercised?	Yes	No
Loss on exercise, per $1 principal	SFr(1.8179-1.7480) = SFr0.0699	Nil
Premium payable per $1 principal (in SFr)	p	p
Invest for three months (91 days) at $5^3/_4$% - value becomes	$p\,1 + \frac{(5^3/_4\% \times 91)}{360}$ = 1.0145p	$p\,1 + \frac{(5^3/_4\% \times 91)}{360}$ = 1.0145p
Hedge by purchasing forward $h per $1 principal. Forward rate = 1.7480	Profit in SFr = h(1.8179-1.7480) = 0.0699h	Loss in SFr = h(1.7480-1.6808) = 0.0672h

For breakeven when the spot rate at expiry is 1.6808, the loss on the hedge must equal the value of the premium plus interest, i.e.

1.0145p = 0.0672h .... (1)

For breakeven when the spot rate at expiry is 1.8179, the loss on the option must be equaled by the value of the premium plus the profit on the hedge, i.e.

-0.0699 + 1.0145p + 0.0699h = 0 ... (2)

Substituting (1) in (2)

$$-0.0699 + 0.0672h + 0.0699h = 0$$
$$0.1371h = 0.0699$$
$$h = 0.5098, \text{ say } 0.51$$

Substituting h = 0.51 in equation (1)

$$1.0145p = 0.0672 \times 0.51$$
$$p = 0.0338$$

The minimum premium (p) should be about SFr0.0338 per $1 principal. For a call option of $100,000, this gives a minimum premium of SFr3,380.

The bank should hedge its position by buying forward $50,980 ($100,000 x 0.5098) at 1.7480.

The hedging ratio, h, is the option's delta value. Because the option is at-the-money, we should expect its delta to be around 0.50.

Check

If the spot rate at expiry were 1.8179, the option would be exercised.

	SFr
Option holder buys $100,000 at 1.7480	174,800
Cost of $100,000 spot (1.8179)	181,790
Loss to bank (option writer)	-6,990
Value of premium plus interest (1.0145 x SFr3,380)	+3,430
Cost of buying $50,980 forward (at 1.7480)	89,113
Sale value of $50,980 at spot rate (1.8179)	92,677
Profit on hedge	+3,564

	SFr
Loss on option	-6,990
Value of premium	+3,430
Profit on hedge	+3,564
Net profit (allowing for a rounding error of 4)	0

The Black-Scholes Model

In practise, banks use computers or programable calculators for pricing options. These computer-pricing models are derived from the Black-Scholes model.

A currency option pricing model, for pricing call options and put options on the spot currency, based on the Black-Scholes model, is

$$c = Se^{-rf(t)} N(d_1) - Xe^{-r(t)} N(d_2) \quad \ldots\ldots\ldots\ldots\ldots \quad (1)$$

$$p = Xe^{-r(t)} N(-d_2) - Se^{-rf(t)} N(-d_1) \quad \ldots\ldots\ldots\ldots \quad (2)$$

$$d_1 = \frac{1n(S/X + (r - rf + \frac{\sigma^2}{2})(t)}{\sigma\sqrt{(t)}} \quad \ldots\ldots\ldots\ldots \quad (3)$$

$$d_2 = d_1 \qquad \sigma\sqrt{(t)} \quad \ldots\ldots\ldots\ldots\ldots\ldots\ldots\ldots \quad (4)$$

Where:

c	=	call option premium
p	=	put option premium
S	=	spot exchange rate
X	=	option exercise price (strike price)
r	=	domestic risk-free rate of interest (5% per annum = 0.05, etc.), i.e. the interest rate on government bonds in the currency in which the option premium is payable
rf	=	foreign risk-free rate of interest
t	=	time to expiry, as a proportion of a year (three months = 0.25, etc.)
σ	=	volatility (8% = 0.08, etc.)
e	=	is the natural logarithm constant, 2.71828

ln means natural logarithm value of

$N(d_1)$ means the cumulative normal distribution for the value d_1

$N(d_2)$ means the cumulative normal distribution for the value d_2

The application of this formula will be illustrated with an example.

Example
The options pricing model could be used to calculate a premium using the data given in the exercise above, but with the premium payable in dollars and an at-the-money-spot strike price of 1.7366.

Option Dollar call against Swiss francs
European option
Principal $100,000
Premium payable in dollars
Strike price SFr1.7366 = $1
Expiry: after three months

When option written:

Spot rate	1.7366
Three-month SFr interest rate	$5^3/_4$% (5.75%)
Three-month $ interest rate	$3^1/_8$% (3.125%)
12-month volatility	8%

Analysis
The base currency is the dollar because the premium is payable in dollars. The foreign currency is the Swiss franc.

A three-month option has a time to expiry of 0.25 years, therefore t = 0.25.

$$d_2 = \frac{1n(1.7366/1.7366) + \left[0.03125 - 0.0575 + \frac{0.08^2}{2}\right]0.25}{0.08\sqrt{0.25}}$$

$$= \frac{1n(1.0) + (-0.02305)0.25}{0.08(0.5)}$$

$$= \frac{0 - 0.0057625}{0.04} = -0.1440625$$

$d_2 = -0.1440625 - 0.08\sqrt{25}$

$= -0.14406225 - 0.04$

$= -0.1840625$

The cumulative normal distribution points at -0.1440625 and -0.1840625 give the following values:

$N(d_1) = 0.4427$

$N(d_2) = 0.4270$

$c = (1.7366e^{-0.0575(0.25)}\ 0.4427) - (1.7366e^{-0.03125(0.25)}\ 0.4270)$

$= (1.7366 \times 0.9857 \times 0.4427) - (1.7366 \times 0.9922 \times 0.4270)$

$= 0.7578 - 0.7357$

$= 0.0221$

The premium is \$0.0221 per \$1 of underlying currency, or \$2,210 in total (0.0221 x \$100,000).

Assumptions in the Black-Scholes Model

Options models based on the Black-Scholes formula incorporate various assumptions. These include

- the riskless hedge principle. An option writer can hedge against changes in the value of an option by buying or selling the underlying instrument, to eliminate risk. In the case of currency options, an option writer can create a riskless hedge by buying or selling forward the underlying currency
- there is a risk-free rate of interest for borrowing/investing each currency
- the exchange rate, i.e. the price of the underlying instrument, will change continually, but will not suffer sharp rises or falls
- changes in the exchange rate, i.e. volatility in the price of the underlying instrument, have a log-normal distribution.

Glossary

American Option

Option contract that can be exercised at any time up to its expiry date.

At-the-money

A currency option's strike price is at-the-money when it is equal to the current exchange rate. At-the-money spot (ATMS) is a strike price equal to the current spot rate. At-the-money forward (ATMF) is a strike price equal to the current forward exchange rate for the same exercise/ maturity date. An American option is said to be at-the-money when it is ATMS and a European option is at-the-money when it is ATMF.

Black-Scholes

A mathematical model or formula for calculating the appropriate premium for a currency option.

Call Option or Currency Option

An option that gives its holder the right to buy a specified quantity of one currency in exchange for another at a stated rate of exchange at some time in the future, on or before expiry date.

Class of Options

Exchange-traded options of the same type, call or put, and style, American or European, for the same currency.

Covered Call Option Writing

For currency options, a situation whereby a dealer writes call options and already possesses the currency to meet the call, or is certain of receiving currency on or prior to the option's expiry date that can be used to meet the call, should the options be exercised.

Cylinder Strategy
Options trading strategy involving both purchasing an option and also writing an option to offset the cost of the purchase. Potential gains therefore are limited.

Delta Hedge
A mathematically based system used by currency options traders to adjust the level of their hedge against currency risk from their options trading position. The system enables a trader to decide how to adjust the hedge in response to changes in the exchange rate.

Derivative
A financial security, such as an option, swap or future, whose value is derived in part from the value and characteristics of another underlying security. In the case of currency swaps and futures, the underlying security is a foreign exchange transaction in the cash FX markets.

European Option
Option contract that can be exercised only on its expiry date.

Exercising a Currency Option
To call on the right to buy (call option) or sell (put option) the currency in the option agreement, obliging the option writer to sell (call option) or buy (put option) the currency at the exercise price.

Exercise Price
Also called the strike price or strike rate. For currency options this is the exchange rate at which the currency can be bought (call option) or sold (put option).

Expiry Month or Expiration Month
The month in which an option expires. Used to identify a series of traded options.

Expiry Date or Expiration Date
The last date on which an option can be exercised. For exchange-traded options this is the Friday/Saturday before the third Wednesday in the expiry month.

Hedge
Take action to reduce or limit a financial risk such as a currency exposure to an adverse exchange rate movement.

Holder
Purchaser of an option.

In-the-money
A currency option's strike price is in-the-money when it is more favorable to the option holder than the current spot market exchange rate (American option) or the forward exchange rate for the same exercise/expiry date (European option). If an option is in-the-money at expiry, it will be exercised unless, in the case of an American option, it has been exercised at an earlier date.

Intrinsic Value
With time value, intrinsic value makes up the premium or purchase price of an option. Intrinsic value is the amount by which the option is in-the-money and is the difference between the strike price and the currency spot market exchange rate.

Liquidation
Any transaction that unwinds or closes out a long or short position.

Liquidity
A market is liquid when it has a high level of trading activity, allowing buying and selling with minimum price changes for individual transactions.

Long Position

In currency trading, a position in which a trader is a net buyer of a currency.

Naked Writing of Call Options

Also called uncovered writing. For currency options, a situation whereby a dealer writes call options, and does not yet possess the currency to meet the call, should the option be exercised. A naked call writer has an exposure in the currency of the call option.

Out-of-the-money

A currency option's strike price is out-of-the-money when it is less favorable to the option holder than the current spot rate of exchange (American option) or the forward rate for the same expiry/maturity date (European options). If an option is out-of-the-money on its expiry date, it will not be exercised.

Premium

The price of an option contract, payable for the purchase of the option.

Put Option or Currency Option

An option that gives its holder the right to sell a specified quantity of one currency in exchange for another at a stated rate of exchange, at some time in the future on or before an expiry date.

Series

A series of exchange-traded options consists of all options of the same class with the same strike price and the same expiry date.

Short Position

Opposite of a long position. In currency trading, a position in which a trader is a net seller of a currency.

Speculator
An investor who seeks to make profits by buying and selling contracts in anticipation of future changes in market prices.

Strike Price or Strike Rate
*See **Exercise Price**.*

Style of Option
Distinction between American and European options.

Time Value
With intrinsic value, time value makes up the premium or purchase price of an option. Time value is that part of the premium that can be attributed to factors such as the time to expiry date and uncertainty about exchange rate movements or volatility over that time. Time value can be measured as the difference between the premium and the intrinsic value.

Type of Option
Distinction between call and put options.

Volatility
Measurement/description of price variability in the underlying security. For currency options and futures, volatility refers to the historical or potential future movements in the spot exchange rate.

Volume
The number of transactions, buy or sell only, in a contract made during a specified time period, typically one trading day.

Writer
Seller of an option contract.

Index

Notes

Notes

Notes

Notes

Notes

Notes